My

Seven Essential Daily Prayers

A Retired Pastor's Journey
Into a Powerful
Personal Focus in Prayer

(Originally published as *Seven Essential Daily Prayers: Build a Firewall Every Morning for Your Spiritual Survival*)

Updated and Revised
June 2020

Loren L Fenton, D.Min.

A Product of GoodlifeNews! Productions
College Place, Washington, USA
https://goodlifenews.co

Requests to publish work from this book should be sent to:
Loren@LorenFentonAuthor.com

Cover Art Photo Credit: Stock Photo from
https://BookBrush.com

Cover Designed using Book Brush online app

ISBN: 978-1-7351365-0-9

Dedication

First: *to the God of Heaven who both hears and answers the sincere heart-felt prayers of every soul at any time day or night. He is always there.*

Second: *To the sacred memory of my mother, Oral D. (Wilson) Fenton who taught me from my "cradle days" the value and joy of telling Jesus about all the concerns of life, large or small.*

Third: *To the memory of Elder Glenn Coon, whose books and ministry in the "ABC Prayer Crusade" made a profound impact on my personal prayer life.*

Fourth: *To the innumerable "prayer warriors" I have known and admired in their passion for teaching Spirit-filled living to the family of God.*

Contents

Acknowledgments
Specific to this second edition of
Seven Essential Daily Prayers

First: There are not enough words to thank my wife Ruth, the love of my life, chief encourager, patient listener, wise counselor, and number one raving fan. What a lady! My joy in her is truly boundless.

Second: I am eternally grateful for the kind, patient teachers who guided my learning experience from early elementary school through high school, college, and grad school. They have formed my life in countless moments of insight, instruction, and encouragement.

Third: The primary revision needed in the first version of Seven Essential Daily Prayers *was kindly pointed out to me by Ed Lindsay, manager of the Auburn ABC, Auburn WA. His gracious observation opened the door to republishing* SEDP *under the current title and sub-title. I appreciated his gentle suggestion for improving the book. I trust the changes, though minor, will result in a more satisfying experience for each reader.*

Introduction

Prayer has always been an important part of my life. When I was very young, my mother taught me to "talk to Jesus" every night when she tucked me into bed. I grew up attending church, and early on I was often asked to lead our church youth group in prayer. At home, our family paused to pray before every meal three times a day. My turn to "say grace" at the table happened regularly.

The idea of prayer was such an integral part of our lives that I didn't think very much about it. That changed when I was about half-way through my teenage years.

One night when I was sixteen, I had a hard time settling down for the night. I tossed and turned on my bed for an hour or more, but sleep wouldn't come. Everyone else was already chasing dreamland fantasies, but not me. Our big old farmhouse was lighted only by faint moonlight streaming through the windows. Everything was quiet—except for the heavy breathing of my slumbering family.

I often went for nighttime walks, so on that night when sleep wouldn't come it was not unusual for me to get up, get dressed, and head out the back door. I glanced up at the clear sky and shining moon and began walking along a lane that led to the fields of our farm. It was a beautiful night, a cool evening with a gentle, almost imperceptible breeze.

Out there, under the moon and stars, I began to talk with God.

I was no stranger to prayer, but this time was different. God was talking to me! There was no physical presence I could touch with my hands, but I could truly feel Him walking beside me. There were no audible words—except mine—but I knew when He spoke to my heart.

I gazed up into the star-studded sky.

"Jesus," I said, "tonight I accept you as my personal Savior and invite you to be Lord of my life. I open my heart's door to you. Please come into my heart and live in me!"

In all the years of religion through my childhood and youth, never once had I taken this step. But that night, alone on that dusty lane under the moon and stars, that prayer became an anchoring milestone in my spiritual journey.

"Lord, what do you want me to do with my life?" I asked.

At that moment I heard God's voice inviting me to a lifetime of Christian ministry. The compass of my life was reset to highways and byways I could never have imagined. Now, nearly six decades later, I look back with amazement. On that dusty road my first baby steps of personal faith began a journey that continues even to this day.

In June 2011 I retired from 40 years of pastoral ministry.

I didn't know it that evening when I walked that moonlit path, but—looking back—I can see God's hand at work, leading, guiding, and empowering my walk with Him—and teaching me new lessons in prayer all along the way.

By early December after retiring, I had decided to reconnect with my blue-collar roots by leasing out my Dodge Ram pickup truck to deliver fifth-wheel RVs and travel trailers from factories to dealerships for their market. I genuinely enjoyed my "owner-operator" status in this tiny niche of the trucking industry. The job involved many, many miles of driving—and many hours of solitary reflection—as I traveled the highways of America and Canada. I was blessed to see some incredibly beautiful places, and I often found myself praising God all for the beauty of His Creation.

But the devil was out there on the road with me, too. At times during those long hours of getting from one place to another, I found my mind wandering into unhealthy areas of imagination. I knew that indulging in impure thoughts would sow bitter seeds of tragic loss in my spiritual experience and could inevitably destroy everything I held dear if I allowed them to grow. The fruit would be bitter, indeed. There's no way I wanted to go there!

The only recourse I had was prayer. I spoke right out loud—right there in the cab of my truck—traveling sixty-miles-per-hour on the freeway, with a 38' fifth-wheel trailer behind me.

"Lord," I cried, "I want purity in my mind! I don't want these evil thoughts. I reject them, and I pray for the purity that only you can give!"

To my utter amazement, immediately my thoughts were freed from the devil's trap, and I could focus once again on healthy, life-building matters.

Over the next several months that simple prayer for purity expanded with several more. I began adding "righteousness in my heart," and "integrity for my life" every time another tempting thought would rear its ugly head. And each time, God graciously delivered me by removing those errant, dark imaginations and replacing them with hope, peace, and light.

Eventually, I began to sense that God was taking me into a new journey I never anticipated. Those basic three prayers—purity, righteousness, and integrity— were joined by another four: "joy for my spirit," "strength for my body," "wisdom for my counsel," and "to be a godly influence in the world." These seven became my personal "essential daily prayers." Of course, my prayers are never restricted to those seven only, but they are where I still begin my day, every day. I cannot survive spiritually without making this vital connection with God.

Watching the progressive growth and development of this journey has been wonderfully exciting. I have presented my experience and the ideas of the *Seven Essential Daily Prayers* series in live devotionals, and numerous sermons. At this writing there is also a retreat-type seven-session seminar in the visioning stage.

And, now this book.

My deepest prayer of all is that every reader of these pages might find a rich personal walk with God, a vibrant spiritual journey, an abiding hunger for purity and righteousness, and to be filled with the Creator's Agápe love.

Loren L. Fenton

2020

Introduction to the Supplemental Study Guide Materials

for

My Seven Essential Daily Prayers

The Study Guide questions, and journal pages placed at the end of each chapter are designed to be used in personal devotions by individuals studying alone, or in group discussions where several people mutually seek spiritual enrichment.

To get you started, I've placed a beginning set of general questions here ahead of Chapter One. Following each chapter is another set of questions and a few pages to record your thoughts.

I hope that each reader will find encouragement, depth, and inspiration in these suggested questions.

General Questions

1. If you knew that today was your last day on Earth, what would you be doing right now?

2. Which do you consider more important:

    > 2.1. Striving for personal righteousness so you will be ready to meet Jesus at his second coming; or

    > 2.2. Responding in loving acts to the needs of other people around you?

3. What temptations seem to slam you at inconvenient or unguarded moments?

4. What do you need to so you can have a consistent time alone with God every day?

5. Are there factors in your life you need to surrender to God right now? What, if anything, is holding you back from yielding those thoughts/issues/habits to Him?

Your Thoughts

_____

_____

_____

_____

_____

_____

_____

_____

_____

Chapter One

Purity in My Mind

That God's Agápe Love May Live in Me

A carrier of light must never be a practitioner of darkness. – LLF

Rome, Italy, c. A.D.66-67. An old man shivers as he sits alone, surrounded by cold stone walls in Rome's Mamertine Prison dungeon. This once-upon-a-time cistern constructed six centuries earlier and located near the Forum, functions as a holding cell for political prisoners and mortal enemies of the Empire. Saul of Tarsus, as he is still known by Roman authorities, glances up at the large round hole in the ceiling above him. It's the only way in or out of this terrible place. He doesn't have much time left, he knows. Roman citizens convicted of sedition were usually beheaded in the public square. He hopes the next time he's lifted by ropes up through that hole will bring him exoneration and freedom, but he knows that it could very well be his last exit from life itself.

The Apostle Paul's thoughts, however, are far from his current misery or his impending fate. Angels of God have visited him there in the dungeon, warming his heart and bringing an indescribable peace. He thinks of his young associate Timothy, working hard and doing his best to oversee the church at Ephesus, more than a thousand miles east of Rome.

One of the few privileges Paul does have is the freedom to write. Did he have a table and chair with writing materials, even in that awful hell hole? Did he dictate his message to a scribe? I'm not sure. But, one way or another he is able to get a letter composed and sent on its way to Timothy. It's a message of encouragement, promise, hope, and instruction.

Paul paints no rosy picture of the challenges facing Timothy in the task of proclaiming the gospel and leading the church in that city. As a result of Paul's ministry there, thousands of people rioted for two whole hours in defense of their goddess Diana, screaming "Great is Diana of the Ephesians!"[1]

Sitting there in that Roman dungeon, Paul proclaims with a prophetic pen: "Things are going to get a whole lot worse before they get better" (my feeble paraphrase).

But Paul's vision is more than just for Ephesus. There in that ancient Roman prison God opens the eyes of His faithful servant to future social conditions wherever and whenever believers worship the God of heaven.

With prophetic pen the Apostle describes "the last days" to Timothy: "People," he says, "will be narcissistic, greedy, profane, hateful, disrespectful, treacherous, uncontrollable, and blasphemous."[2]

It doesn't take a Ph.D. to realize—we're there.

The good news in Paul's prophecy is that the "last days" means Jesus will very soon make another personal appearance on this planet! He's not coming this time as a helpless newborn baby in a first-century Bethlehem barn. This time he's coming as King of kings, and Lord of lords. All the angels of heaven come with him, shouting, blowing

---

[1] Acts 19:28, 34

[2] See 2 Timothy 3:1-5

trumpets, opening graves. The risen saints of all ages spring forth with brand new, glorified bodies, claiming victory over death and the grave. They are joined by a vast throng of the living saved who blend their voices in joyous exclamations of hosannas and hallelujahs. What a day that will be![3]

But, what does all this have to do with "Purity in My Mind," the first prayer in *My Seven Essential Daily Prayers*?

It all goes back to one of the Beatitudes Jesus spoke in his Sermon on the Mount. With a crowd of fishermen, farmers, and other commoners pressed in close to catch every word, he said, "Blessed are the pure in heart, *for they shall see God"*. (Matthew 5:8 emphasis mine).

I believe that means we will see him with our own living eyes, not just to "see" as in "understanding."

The Apostle John, in the Book of Revelation, says, "Behold, he is coming with clouds, and every eye will see him, even they who pierced him" (Revelation 1:7).

And, again, the angels who spoke to Jesus' disciples gazing into the sky where they last saw him, gave them this great assurance: "This same Jesus, who was taken up from you into heaven, will

---

[3] See 1 Thessalonians 4:13-18

so come in like manner as you saw him go into heaven" (Acts 1:11).

One more beautiful promise: *[The servants of God] will serve him (in the New Earth). They shall see His face![4]*

I want to see Jesus like that!

Here's why purity of mind and heart are an absolute condition of salvation: *Believers with pure hearts will see God because they are filled with God's love.*

A pure heart empowers and produces God's *Agápe* love.

In the Apostle Paul's first letter to Timothy, he told him, "The goal . . . is [*Agápe*] love, which comes from a pure heart and a good conscience and a sincere faith" (1 Timothy 1:5).

Did you notice that? The *goal of purity* is to *provide the soil where God's* Agápe *love can grow.*

Agápe love is the very heart of the gospel. It is the central theme of the entire Bible from Genesis to Revelation. It is the great motivating element in the heart of God, yearning over his wayward children. "For God so *loved* the world that he gave his only begotten Son, that whoever believes in him

---

[4] Revelation 22:3-4

should not perish but have everlasting life" (John 3:16 emphasis supplied).

The greatest statement about *Agápe* love also comes from the Apostle Paul, "And now these three remain: faith, hope, and love. But the greatest of these is love" (1 Corinthians 13:13).[5]

Agápe love was the nuclear core of Jesus' teaching, and the quality he most desired to see in his disciples. He said, "A new commandment I give to you, that you love [*agápe*] one another; as I have loved you, that you also love one another. By this all will know that you are my disciples, if you have love for one another" (John 13:34, 35).

But what, specifically, is a*gápe* love? How is it different from any other kind of love? Why is it so important that we have this special kind of love ruling in our minds and hearts?

Let's find out.

In 336 B.C. at the age of 20, Alexander III of Macedon succeeded his father Phillip II as king. By the time Alexander ("the Great") died a scant twelve years later—in 323 B.C—he had forged an empire so massive it extended from the eastern shores of the Adriatic Sea to the Indus River 3,200 miles to the east, and south to the upper reaches of

---

[5] The entire chapter of 1 Corinthians 13 is unparalleled in its beauty, simplicity, and profound understanding of agápe love. I highly recommend memorizing this passage of Scripture.

the Nile in Southern Egypt. By 356 B.C. some 70 cities across that vast territory bore his name and were ruled by garrisons of Greek soldiers. Over the next two hundred years Greek language and culture permeated every corner of the Empire, influencing everything from religious practices to entire social networks. Koiné Greek became a common language bridging the gap separating all the many diverse conquered nations.

The Greeks recognized three different kinds of love. They had different names for each. By the time the New Testament was written (using Greek) in the 1st century A.D., these three names for "love" were as commonly known and used as much as we might talk about the three forms of H_2O (solid, liquid, gas) today.

Here are the three Greek words for "love":

Eros—**physical (sensual, sexual) love.** From *eros* we get our current English word "erotic." For the ancient Greeks—and New Testament authors—this did not carry the taboos or social stigmas that it often does today. It simply was a way to express the element of physical arousal and attraction in human relationships.

Philos—**Brotherly love; friendship.** The American city of Philadelphia, Pennsylvania was named to carry the identity "The City of Brotherly Love." *Philos* is the bonding love of friends, or soldiers in a tight-knit unit, or kids who have grown up together and maintain their connection well into adulthood because of loyalty, common experiences, and just because they still like to hang out with each other.

Agápe—Love as a principle; Godly love; unconditional; unbroken. The best example of *Agápe* is found in John 3:16, "For God so loved the world that he gave his one and only Son, that whoever believes in him shall not perish but have eternal life."

The devil hates *Agápe* love! In our age he has brought out all the big guns in his arsenal to do everything in his power to demolish it. *Agápe* love is the heart of God and is the very first fruit of God's Holy Spirit dwelling in a believer's heart.[6] In Satan's eyes *agápe* must be relentlessly attacked and destroyed. He knows that by destroying God's love in our hearts he can break our bond with God and His gift of eternal life. The Apostle Peter warns, "Be self-controlled and alert. Your enemy the devil prowls around like a roaring lion looking for someone to devour" (1 Peter 5:8).

The evil foe of heaven knows that *the most effective way to eliminate true, godly love in the human heart is to destroy purity.* For this reason, our first line of defense—the very first building block for our wall of spiritual survival—must be to pray for purity in our thought life. Thoughts become imaginations, and if allowed to grow, imaginations become desires, desires become resolutions, resolutions become actions. If we act out those

[6] See Galatians 5:22

ungodly thoughts, we sin, and the devil's forces win the battle.

Make no mistake. This battle is very, very real.

Our world today is a moral swampland. Social media, cable television, pop music, and magazines spew non-stop sleaze and hyper-sexed programming into the minds of young and old alike. Internet porn sites are visited more than Netflix, Amazon, and Twitter combined! A recent report stated that over 70% of the American population are porn consumers! It is impossible to avoid. Even the advertisements capitalize on the allure of illicit indulgence.

In truth, this rampant immorality is nothing new. It's been around since before Noah and the biblical Flood.

The Lord saw how great man's wickedness on the earth had become, and that every inclination of his heart was only evil all the time. The Lord was grieved that he had made man on the earth, and his heart was filled with pain. So, the Lord said, "I will wipe mankind, whom I have created, from the face of the earth—men and animals, and creatures that move along the ground, and birds of the air—for I am grieved that I have made them." But Noah found grace in the eyes of the Lord" (Genesis 6:5-8).

In the first century A.D., James, the brother of Jesus wrote to the church, "Pure and undefiled religion before God and the Father is this: to visit orphans and widows in their trouble, and to keep oneself unspotted from the world" (James 1:27).

In all reverence I ask, *How in the Name of the Lord are we supposed to do that?*

Let's admit it. We've all drunk the swamp water. Paul defines our situation clearly when he says, "All have sinned and come short of the glory of God" (Romans 3:23). A few verses earlier in the same chapter he quotes several Old Testament prophets from a thousand years earlier: "There is none righteous, not even one; there is none who understands, no one who seeks God. All have turned away, they have together become worthless; there is no one who does good, not even one" (Romans 3:10-12).[7]

The Prophet Isaiah agrees. He declares: "All our righteousnesses are as filthy rags" (Isaiah 64:6).

The bottom line of all this is: We can *never* win the quest for moral purity in this life in our own strength. Not by willpower. Not by determination. Not by force of personality. Not even by senility! Our only hope is in the power of the Holy Spirit filling us with his presence. But that truly is good news! Survival is possible!

God's amazing grace gives us hope.

---

[7] (See also Psalm 14:1-3; 53:1-3; Ecclesiastes 7:20)

"The wages of sin is death, but the gift of God is eternal life in Christ Jesus our Lord" (Romans 6:23). When we accept Jesus Christ as our personal Savior and Lord, we receive our new life in him. "Therefore, if anyone is in Christ, he is a new creation; the old has gone, the new has come! (2 Corinthians 5:17).

That new life in Christ is, in fact, eternal life. It begins now, even before we get to heaven. When we are "in Christ," and Christ is "in us," we have Christ's righteousness and purity in our mind and heart because Jesus lives in us via the Holy Spirit. "Jesus was tempted an all points as we are, yet without sin" (Hebrews 4:15). Therefore, it is *Christ in [us], [which gives us] the hope of glory* (Colossians 1:27b, emphasis supplied), even right now, today.

The big question, however, is How do we maintain our new life in Christ? With temptations multiplied every day on every hand, how do we even get through an hour—let alone a whole day or a lifetime—with this new life intact?

First, *we walk by faith and not by sight* (2 Corinthians 5:7 NKJV). Nevertheless, here are some "living-the-life" principles from the Bible, written for our encouragement:

Philippians 2:5 *Let this mind be in you which was also in Christ Jesus* (NKJV).

21

Psalm 119:9 *How can a young [person] keep his way pure? By living according to Your word.*

Psalm 119:11 *Your word I have hidden in my heart, that I might not sin against you* (NKJV).

So, while we recognize that spiritual purity is totally and completely a gift from God, nevertheless the individual choices we make are crucial to successfully living for him. Certain routines and habits contribute mightily to preserving the peace with God we receive in Christ. Purity is a gift. Maintaining purity is a choice. God gives the victory. We live the victory by our choices.

Here is a key habit/routine for living the promise:

Set a specific time every morning before you get into the busyness of the day to read something from the Bible. There are many Bible-reading plans available. Using a plan you get from another source is fine, or you can design your own plan. It doesn't matter. Your plan may be to study a specific subject or focus on a special passage, or it may be as simple as beginning with Genesis 1:1 and reading straight through to Revelation 22:21. That's the plan I've personally followed since beginning my Christian journey at age sixteen. As I write this, I am now less than two weeks away from my 75th birthday, and—with God's grace and blessing—I am nearing the end of my 41st trip through the Word. And all I can say is, God is faithful, God is good, God is love.

Spend some time in quiet contemplation—meditation—on the passage(s) you read.

Memorize some scriptural promises. In this way you will internalize the power of God's Word, giving you strength for the day to resist and overcome the devil's temptations.

Finally, brothers, whatever is noble, whatever is right, whatever is pure, whatever is lovely, whatever is admirable—if anything is excellent or praiseworthy—think about such things (Philippians 4:8).

Remember, a heart of purity empowers godly, unconditional, unbroken *Agápe* love.

The enemy's goal is to break the bond of love between us, our fellowman, and God.

We are all guilty of drinking the devil's swamp water, but God's Word is a resource for redemption and restoration.

By our freewill choice we receive God's gift of love, forgiveness, and moral power.

Study Guide

Chapter One
"Purity in My Mind"

*Moral Purity is the Catalyst for
God's Agápe Love to Thrive in
our Hearts*

1. How do you think the Apostle Paul
    could spiritually endure the
    horrors of imprisonment, torture,
    and even the threat of death by a
    Roman executioner's ax?

2. Is it possible to purge your mind
    of evil thoughts simply by thinking
    about other things?

3. What does "agápe" love mean to you?
    How can you experience "agápe"
    love?

4. Since "all have sinned and come short of the glory of God," how can we ever find true purity of heart and mind?

5. What role does personal freewill choice have in a person's quest for righteous living?

Your Thoughts

_____

_____

_____

_____

_____

_____

_____

_____

_____

_____

Chapter Two

Righteousness in My Heart

That I May be Filled with God's Holy Spirit

> *Blessed are those who hunger and thirst for righteousness, for they will be filled. - Matthew 5:6*

MOUNT EREMOS, GALILEE, ISRAEL, February 1997—I absolutely couldn't help myself. Collapsing onto the ground I sat and sobbed like a baby. I blinked back my tears, drinking in the scene around me. No one else was nearby, but not far away I noticed other pastors from our tour group also deeply emotional. Some silently wept in the awesome wonder of that wonderful moment on the mountain.

Winter rains were over, at least on that day. Fluffy white clouds drifted lazily across a bright blue sky, sailing east from the distant Mediterranean toward Jordan, Saudi Arabia, and Iraq. A springtime feel dominated everything. Birds sang. Early flowers were budding. The grounds of the Franciscan chapel—built near this traditional site of the Sermon on the Mount—were groomed to perfection. Just to the north, adjacent to the church property, a broad gentle valley sloped southward toward the valley floor. The formation of the landscape could easily accommodate several thousand people sitting in nature's open-air theater. The acoustics were phenomenal. If everybody was quietly listening, a speaker at the bottom of the hill could easily be heard and understood by the entire crowd. It was easy to think of Jesus speaking to people in that very spot.

A vibrant, living green covered the surrounding hills. Below us, the Lake of Gennesaret (Sea of Galilee) stretched away to the south, emptying into the Jordan River on its journey to the Dead Sea.

I caught my breath, thinking back to my early years as a young farm boy growing up in Washington State's Yakima Valley. Those same-looking fluffy white clouds often drifted across our farm in springtime, dotting the sagebrush hills flanking the valley to the north and south with great shadows moving across the landscape. The blue sky of Israel reminded me of our deep blue sky at home. The sparkling beauty of the lake spoke to me of the great Pacific Northwest.

Something deep inside me opened a knowledge of God's love that day such as I had never encountered before. At least not like this.

For some strange reason, which I have yet to understand, that experience became another epiphany for me—a living encounter with the living God. Without spoken words, I heard my inner voice responding, *Jesus knows me! He understands me! He grew up and lived in this place so like my own early years. Yes, Jesus knows and understands me! And he loves me!*

No chairs or benches were anywhere nearby. All I could do was drop to the ground and sit cross-legged, weeping in the fullness of my spirit. No words are adequate to describe my soaring joy.

I've thought about that trip so often since then. The wonder has never ceased.

I can well imagine Jesus looking out across that body of blue water, perhaps glancing toward the rising hills east of the lake. Over there, settlements of mostly Greek heritage dotted the shoreline. Non-Jews felt no restrictions on raising pigs. The area swarmed with herds numbering into the thousands. I wonder if that day on the mountain if Jesus may have thought about those demoniacs in the region of the Gergesenes whom he would soon set free from their captivity.[8] I wonder if he, even then, heard their desperate cry for deliverance, their hearts hungering for righteousness and peace.

I wonder if Jesus may also have thought about the story he would share later about the boy who left home with his inheritance, only to find himself herding pigs for a farmer "in a far country."[9] That area east of Galilee could well have been the place.

The boy was just a kid. Maybe late teens, early twenties. You know the story. Kid gets bored with farm life, asks his dad for his inheritance, gets it, and heads out to find a life of excitement. After blowing all his wealth on wine, women, and song he finds himself a long way from home, broke, abandoned, starving in a pigsty, and wishing he could eat very the husks the animals have. In a flash of brilliant insight, the kid realizes the stupidity of his situation, leaves the pigs, hits the road. He's going home. Dad sees him coming from a great distance away, drops everything, and rushes— runs!—to embrace his boy. Tears flow. Party time! Celebrate! Kill the fatted calf! The boy is back!

We don't know all the details about this boy and his family, of course. The location of their farm, for instance. And, where—exactly—did the kid go

---

[8] See Matthew 8.

[9] See Luke 15:11-32

when he hit the road for his grand adventure? Jesus didn't say. But it's not hard to imagine some definite possibilities.

Jesus grew up in Nazareth of Galilee. The rich soil and generally mild climate of Galilee made farming and agriculture a mainstay of the area's economy. Just to the north of Nazareth—about 5 miles away, or an hour's walk—sat the city of Sepphoris. Around the time of Jesus' birth in Bethlehem, Herod Antipas began to rebuild Sepphoris as the capital city of Galilee. The process took many years. As the city grew in importance and the population swelled, the needs for builders, craftsmen, and a steady, reliable source of foodstuffs and other supplies increased by the day. Could it be that Joseph took his carpentry skills and his young adopted son Jesus to Sepphoris where work opportunities were plentiful? They could have even commuted—walking the ten-mile round trip every day—leading a donkey loaded with their tools. It's not outside the realm of possibility.

Perhaps on those trips to the city, or maybe in the Sepphorian marketplace, the young Jesus met and became acquainted with a farm family with two sons roughly his age, bringing their produce to sell? We don't know this, of course. It's all pure speculation. But, it's not impossible. For me—even though it's completely imaginary—it provides a wonderful backstory for Jesus' parable of the lost boy in Luke 15.

On the day at the beginning of his ministry when Jesus gave the Sermon on the Mount, I can't help but wonder if, as he glanced away toward the eastern shore of the Sea of Galilee, he might have been thinking about a friend from his youth. A friend whom he loved, but who had chosen to leave the warm security of home and hearth, chasing excitement in the pagan Greek cities of the Decapolis where he soon hit rock bottom in a pigpen, but who then returned home to a welcome of love, acceptance, and restoration. I like to think so.

One thing is for sure. That young "Prodigal Son" realized while sitting among those pigs that all the exciting thrills money can buy cannot satisfy the heart. It wasn't just the emptiness of his stomach that drove him to go. It was the aching hunger for home and family. He understood his sins for what they were and immediately determined to confess them to his father.

And his father accepted him! Love and grace won the day, and lavish gifts poured from the rejoicing father's heart. His own robe. His own ring. His own sandals for the barefoot boy. Strike up the band. It's time to sing and dance. "This, my son," he cries, "was dead and is alive again; he was lost and is found! (Luke 15:32).

Jesus looks at the waiting crowd on the mountainside and begins to teach.

- *Blessed are the poor in spirit, for theirs is the kingdom of heaven.*

- *Blessed are those who mourn, for they will be comforted.*

- *Blessed are the meek, for they will inherit the earth.*

- *Blessed are those who hunger and thirst after righteousness, for they will be filled.*

- *Blessed are the merciful, for they will be shown mercy.*

- *Blessed are the pure in heart, for they will see God.*

- *Blessed are the peacemakers, for they will be called the sons of God.*

- *Blessed are those who are persecuted because of righteousness, for theirs is the kingdom of heaven* (Matthew 5:3-10).

Did you notice that awesome promise right in the middle of those eight beatitudes? "Blessed are those who hunger and thirst after righteousness, *for they will be filled!* (Matthew 5:6, Emphasis supplied).

I read those words and realize how hungry I am. Not just hungry—I'm starving! I'm totally empty. My natural spiritual heart is weak and fainting. I can't even stand up on my own. If I don't get revived, I'll die for sure.

In the previous chapter, "Purity in My Mind," we saw what Paul said in his letter to the Romans: "There is none righteous, no, not one" (Romans 3:10).

So, there we are—*wretched, pitiful, poor, blind, and naked* (Revelation 3:17). Quite a picture, isn't it? And, sadly, oh so true.

Those words from Revelation also come directly from Jesus himself, not just to an assembled crowd of farmers and fishermen on a Galilean hillside, but to you and me, right now, today.

Back in Romans, we read, "The kingdom of God is not eating and drinking, but righteousness and peace and joy in the Holy Spirit" (Romans 14:17). A few verses later Paul adds, "Everything that was written in the past was written to teach us, so that through endurance and the encouragement of the Scriptures we might have hope" (Romans 15:4).

Hope! What a powerful word—especially when we're hungry! Jesus promises us in the fourth beatitude that people who hunger and thirst for righteousness will, indeed, be filled. His assurance truly gives us hope, even in our hopelessness.

Let's explore how this works.

Here are three keys that—for me—help unlock the door of God's storehouse filled with abundant grace for our aching needs:

Key #1; Recognize and Embrace the Source of Spiritual Hunger

When I was thirteen years old, I entered my freshman year of high school. Along with nearly all the other boys in our farming community, I enrolled in Vocational Agriculture and became a member of the Future Farmers of America (FFA). A major portion of the VoAg class was spent in shop activities, where we learned various practical skills needed for successful farming—things like welding, carpentry, machinery operation and repair, etc. The shop was well equipped with tools, workstations, and everything needed for us to learn the best practices for modern agriculture through hands-on experience.

One wall of the shop held a large panel displaying all the hand tools anyone would need for a project. Pliers, wrenches, various screwdrivers, hammers and such hung on the board, each with its spot marked by a painted silhouette showing the outline of the tool. Our VoAg teacher, Mr. Chevy Chase, very strictly enforced a rule that every tool must be in its place when the bell rang at the end of class. We were all supposed to return every tool we were using to the board, then we could be dismissed.

Mr. Chase's system worked exceptionally well in preserving the shop's supply of tools and equipment. One day, however, a small pair of pliers slipped into the leg pocket of my coveralls, walked with me right out the door, and found a new home on our farm. No one at school seemed to miss it. Not even Mr. Chase. I felt quite smug because I "got away with it."

Fast forward a couple of years to the night under the stars when I walked and talked with God, giving my life to Him, and heard Him calling me to a lifetime of Christian ministry.[10] Not long after that life-changing encounter with the Holy Spirit my father, my brother, and I were working on a project in our home shop shed. My dad went looking for something in his toolbox and came across a pair of pliers he didn't recognize.

"What are these pliers?" he asked. "I never put them in here. Where'd they come from?"

I didn't say a word, but my brother glared at me with an accusing stare. He didn't tell Dad either, but later he confronted me.

"You stole those pliers from the Ag shop, didn't you!" His tone carried more accusations than a question.

---

[10] See Introduction, pp. 1,2

I still wouldn't admit it, but he continued, "I know you did. I recognize those pliers from school. You stole them and brought them home!"

I didn't say anything, and the conversation was dropped. I honestly don't remember all the exact details of what happened next, but the pliers stayed in their new home. And, other than my brother, I don't think anyone else ever knew. Except there was that little whispering voice in my head that popped up at the most unexpected times telling me, *Thief! You know you stole those pliers. You're as guilty as sin!*

Fast forward again. This time about six more years.

Life was good in the Spring of 1967. I was getting ready to graduate from college with my bachelor's degree in theology. The woman of my dreams—a newly minted Registered Nurse—had agreed to marry me(!), and we were getting excited as our big day in early June grew closer and closer. Immediately after my graduation in August, I would begin pastoral ministry in Portland, Oregon. We had a beautiful brand-new car that we both loved. We were young and alive with hopes and dreams for our future. We both had great jobs—and we both loved Jesus. I don't think life could get any better. Love is grand.

One night we parked under the stars and talked about the life we were entering together, and about the Second Coming of Christ. The greatest event of all ages seemed so near. We both wanted to be ready for Jesus to come soon so we could live eternally with Him in the Earth made new. Our hearts beat as one that evening, swelling with love and hope.

Thief! You know you stole those pliers. You're as guilty as sin!

There was that pesky voice reminding me again of such a little transgression from years before. Why wouldn't it just go away!

Not only that. You also lifted a can of pop from the grocery store that same year. What makes you think you're good enough to go to Heaven?

I took Ruth's hand in mine. "Sweetheart," I began, "There's something I need to do. Years ago, when I was just starting high school, I stole a pair of pliers and a can of pop. I need to go home and make those things right. I don't want to miss out on Heaven for a pair of pliers and a can of pop."

The next day we looked at the calendar and chose an early upcoming date when we could visit my old home 100 miles to the west.

My parents were delighted to see us. Ruth stayed and visited with them while I drove into town. It was a weekday, so I knew school would be in session. I drove into the high school parking lot and found a spot near the VoAg shop and classroom. It seemed like my heart was beating 100 miles per hour.

Mr. Chase was still teaching the same classes all these years later. I saw him sitting at his desk as I entered the classroom and glanced through his office window. A quick knock on the open door brought an instant surprised grin of delight to his face.

"Loren Fenton? What a surprise! Come in and have a seat!" He motioned toward a chair across the desk from his. "What brings you here? It's good to see you!"

"Well," I began, "I came to bring you something." I pulled a new pair of pliers from the bag in my hands and handed them to him. "This is to replace some pliers I took out of the shop when I was here as a student. This has been weighing on my conscience for the last eight years, and I decided I'd better come and make it right."

He shook his head in disbelief.

"Really? That's hard to believe. I never knew. I would never suspect you for doing something like that. But I appreciate you coming. It is encouraging when these things happen."

"I'm sure you've probably had others come with similar confessions," I said.

"Yes, I have," he answered. "But not after eight years!"

The folks at the grocery store were equally as gracious. And, I felt a great weight leave my spirit. It wasn't the value of the items themselves. It was knowing I had done the right thing making restitution for a couple of stupid actions from my youth. That condemning voice in my head was silenced forever about those pliers and that can of pop. I was free!

I also learned a great four-part truth: (A) Sin creates "Spiritual Anxiety," aka "guilt." (B) This Holy Spirit-inspired *guilt* convicts me of my *wrongness*, which (C) creates *remorse*, and (D) leads to *repentance* and *restitution*.

Owning the guilt is the first step toward receiving the fullness of God's promises and power to live a life of righteousness.

Key #2; Personally Accept (by faith) Christ's Righteousness as Your Own

I relate that story above, not to say or imply that two little incidents from my early high school experience are the worst things I ever did, or that we gain God's forgiveness by our works of restitution. Far from it, on both fronts! Sadly, I've had to own and confess far more serious sins more times than I can count. It breaks my heart that my heart still wanders away from God.

But I've discovered that I'm not alone. The Apostle Paul exclaims in Romans, "What a wretched man I am! Who will rescue me from this body of death?" (Romans 7:24). Paul doesn't stop there, however. He immediately answers his question, "Thanks be to God through Jesus Christ our Lord!" (Romans 7:25).

The central theme of Paul's entire ministry was that the only hope for sinners lies in the righteousness of Christ and that as we put our faith and trust in Him, he exchanges His righteousness for our filthy rags of sin. "God made him (Christ) who had no sin to be sin for us, so that in him we might become the righteousness of God."[11]

Jesus said, "For God so loved the world that he gave his one and only Son, that whoever believes in him shall not perish but have eternal life" (John 3:16).

Such a simple truth. Righteousness comes to us not by our efforts, but as a gift from a loving God who cares for each of us personally.

All we must do is accept His gift with thanksgiving and praise. As we trust His promise, He fulfills His promise, "Blessed are those who hunger and thirst for righteousness, for they will be filled" (Matthew 5:6).

---

[11] See 2 Corinthians 5:21

Key #3; Choose Every Day to Live Righteously

Nevertheless, we have choices to make every day. "Do not be deceived; 'Evil company corrupts good habits.' Come back to your senses as you ought, and stop sinning" (1 Corinthians 15:33, 34).

In other words, we can—and must—choose to live for Jesus, and that choosing positive, godly people as our primary friends can help reinforce our decision. We must realize and live by the truth that on our own we are helpless and doomed to failure. Even so, the righteousness of Christ is our all in all.

Thus, the second of the *My Seven Essential Daily Prayers* is, "Righteousness in My Heart."

It is God's loving gift to us for victorious daily life in Him.

Study Guide

Chapter Two
"Righteousness in My Heart"

Righteousness is a Gift to the
Unrighteous
From a Holy Father whose Heart
is Filled with Grace

1. Have you ever had an experience
    when you felt deep in your heart
    that God truly knows, understands,
    and loves YOU? In a few words,
    describe that experience to the
    group, or record your thoughts in a
    journal

2. How did you react/respond to
    Jesus's story about the Prodigal

Son? Do you identify most with . . .

        2.1. The younger brother who took his inheritance and left home;

        2.2. The father who never stopped yearning for his son to return; or

        2.3. The older brother?

3. What values are most important to you? Why?

4. How do you think Christians today should celebrate when a "prodigal" comes home?

5. Have you ever had to go back and "make things right" with someone? Is there something in your past you that you need to take care of? When will you do it?

6. If righteousness is "by faith," why is it important to do whatever we

can to make restitution to those
whom we have harmed in the past?

Your Thoughts:

_____

_____

_____

_____

_____

_____

_____

_____

_____

_____

_____

_____

_____

_____

_____

_____

_____

_____

_____

_____

_____

_____

_____

_____

_____

_____

_____

_____

_____

_____

CHAPTER THREE
Integrity in My Life

That My Witness for God will be Uncompromised

"'You are my witnesses,' declares the Lord, 'and my servant whom I have chosen'" (Isaiah 42:10).

Well, you know from the last chapter that I stole some stuff when I was a kid in high school. It wasn't any big deal by human standards—just a pair of pliers and a can of pop—the pettiest of petty larceny. Certainly not up there with robbing a bank or grand theft auto or something else really serious. Even so, stealing is stealing, and that made me a thief—a breaker of the Eighth Commandment in God's Big Ten: "You shall not steal" (Exodus 20:15).

What relief I felt when I heard my teacher, Mr. Chase say, "You're forgiven!"

I also sensed God's forgiveness as I accepted His gift of Christ's righteousness to replace my guilt. *Amazing Grace, how sweet the sound!*

However, being a thief in the presence of Jesus doesn't have to be a bad thing. It depends entirely on the choices we make. Two thieves were crucified with Jesus on Calvary. One refused to seek mercy and forgiveness, the other found salvation.[12] A sinner's guilt switched crosses that day. One man died in his own sin, a second died as the sin of another, a third man died forgiven, redeemed, and righteous in the sight of Heaven.

That third man made a choice that saved his life for eternity. Even there on the cross he found freedom in Christ.

Sadly, I must admit that I'm not only a thief, I'm also a liar. No, I never lied on the witness stand in court or told a fib to escape punishment. But, then, there's this . . .

OUTLOOK GRADE SCHOOL, MRS. DAVENPORT'S 1ST GRADE CLASSROOM, 1951-1952. Imagine a bunch of lively first graders—I think there were around 30 of us. I still remember my friends. Tony, Paul, Robert, Linda,

---

[12] See Luke 23:39-43

Leon, Judy, Billy, and many more. Our teacher, Mrs. Davenport, was a motherly soul who loved each of us. She even gave each of us a small gift on her birthday! We spent our days with "Dick and Jane" readers, learning numbers, playing outside at recess, and otherwise just being kids. I was a social child, so I enjoyed all the time with other children my age. Every day was filled with busy activities. After lunch we got our mats out of a storage closet and lay on the floor for naps. We all loved school—and Mrs. Davenport. First grade was fun.

Since six-year-olds often like to tell about their family life experiences, Mrs. Davenport provided a weekly time for us to share "news" from home. My classmates reported things like getting a new model airplane for their birthday, going on a vacation trip, or some other wonderful detail. Even things like Mom was going to have a new baby, or the dog had puppies last night. We were free to say whatever we wanted to say.

Except, I didn't have anything to report. Especially not anything unique or exciting. But, I raised my hand anyway. Mrs. Davenport saw me and gave me a turn.

I rose slowly from my chair and stood with slumped shoulders, head bowed, eyes looking at the floor. I pretended to sniffle, and said in a weepy voice, "M-my Daddy d-d-died last night!"

To this day I have no idea how that little nugget of "fake" news spread so rapidly through our farming community. Wildfire in a wheat field driven by a 30 mile-per-hour gale couldn't have gone any faster. Within minutes the phone at our house began ringing, ringing, ringing! Neighbors calling to deliver condolences and messages of support and sympathy to my mother.

"Oh, Mrs. Fenton, I'm so sorry to hear about your husband! If there's anything I can do, just call me."

Naturally, my mother was quite curious as to the source of this strange rumor about her husband.

"Well," she said, "I'm happy to tell you that the report isn't true. Claude is sitting here in the kitchen, quite alive and well. Thank you for calling, but tell me, where did you get this story?"

Then, one-by-one she began to back-trace the gossip line until she learned that her youngest child had spun this wild tale in school during first grade "sharing time."

There was a loving confrontation at the supper table that evening. Along with appropriate corrective measures (I'll leave that to your imagination), I was admonished with a verse from Scripture I never forgot: "Lying lips are an abomination to the Lord" (Proverbs 12:22a KJV).

I assure you, the core life-principle of truthfulness in all things was duly impressed on a little six-year-old boy that night.

Which brings me rather conveniently to the focus of this chapter, "Integrity in My Life."

I've found three main components to integrity: (1) Foundational honesty; (2) Dependability, and (3) Faithfulness.

Foundational Honesty

Through the years I've had fun swapping stories about lessons learned in childhood with one of my long-time friends. John's family were not church people, and he did not become a Christian until his mid-teens while he was away from home at a Christian boarding school. As often happens, after he gave his heart to Jesus his conscience became awakened to incidents of his life which he knew had to be confessed and repaired. One of those meant telling his father about something that had happened repeatedly over several years during his earlier childhood.

I'll let John tell his story:

"Well, here's what happened. As a young kid I had a love for sweets like you wouldn't believe. Candy, gum, cookies—whatever had sugar in it—called my name! I could finish off a six-stick pack of Juicy Fruit gum in about an hour. I guess you could say I was pretty addicted. My "sweet tooth" was strong, alive, and well. I had no idea it wasn't good for me. If I had known, I wouldn't have cared though. If it was sweet, it was good, and I loved it.

"The problem was that if I wanted to get candy from the store I needed money, but I didn't have any. Even so, I knew where I could get some—my dad had a few coins in his dresser. Sometimes he and some friends got together for a game of poker. Their gambling didn't amount to any high stakes—just some loose pocket change to make their game more interesting. Dad kept his "gambling money" in a small box in one of the bedroom dresser drawers. I figured he wouldn't miss the few cents here and there that I needed for my candy fix. And I was right. He never suspected a thing.

I helped myself quite often to that "bank" of easily available cash.

"When I was about 16 or 17, I was away from home at a Christian high school. The atmosphere there was very spiritual compared to my earlier home life. It wasn't that my parents weren't good people, they just weren't spiritual or religious in any way. The administrators, faculty, and staff at this school were different. Through their influence I met the Lord and decided to live my life for him. That was a life-changing milestone.

"Very soon after my conversion those 'candy coins' began to haunt me. I knew that— among other things—I had to tell my dad about what I had done. It wasn't easy, but at the next home leave I approached Dad and confessed to the error of my ways. I was thankful that his response was quite measured and thoughtful.

"At the end of our conversation, I attempted to summarize my feelings.

'Well,' I said, 'I guess honesty is always the best policy.'

"Dad's piercing black eyes drilled me like a laser beam. I knew something intense and important was about to happen. His voice sounded more serious than I had ever heard him speak before.

'Son,' he said, 'honesty is the ONLY policy.'"

Suffice it to say, my friend John never forgot that life lesson. It is still as fresh for him now, decades after the incident, as it was the day it happened.

Some things we never forget!

What an important principle to live by—especially for Christians who claim to represent the God of heaven! The Ninth Commandment says, "You shall not bear false witness against your neighbor" (Exodus 20:16 NKJV).

I have encountered people who are so in the habit of lying that they will lie when the truth would be better for their cause. The first lie recorded in the Bible is the serpent's statement to Eve in the Garden of Eden, "You will not surely die" (Genesis

3:4). Jesus called him (the devil) "the father of lies" (John 8:44).

And, just to be clear, there will be no liars in heaven. Describing God's heavenly city New Jerusalem, John the Revelator writes, "Nothing impure will ever enter it, nor will anyone who does what is shameful or deceitful, but only those whose names are written in the Lamb's book of life" (Revelation 21:27).

If we expect to live with integrity and total honesty there and then, we need to live by those same principles here and now. This life is the practice run for heaven. Integrity is the natural fruit of an impeccable character.

Character is revealed in the daily life transactions we have with the people we encounter along life's pathway. As the Holy Spirit directs our words and actions, our business dealings will be strictly honest. "The Lord abhors dishonest scales, but accurate weights are his delight" (Proverbs 11:1). The Lord delights in you and in your choices to deal truthfully and honestly in all your aspects of your life.

Foundational honesty means living with transparency—what you see is what you get. It means we must not play games using tactics like hidden agendas, one-upmanship tricks, or deliberate attempts to confuse people for the purpose of control.

It also means we must discipline our thinking for intellectual honesty.

Emotions are good. They are given to us by our great Creator. Emotions drive the passion for our goals and intentions. Without them we would get nowhere. But, good decisions—choices—are not based on emotions alone. That is *emotionalism*.

A healthier approach to decision making is combining our emotional drive with objective thinking. Objectively looking at all issues relative to whatever decision we're making will keep us balanced, and result in stronger choices honoring God in everything.[13]

Dependability

Ruth and I have moved quite a few times during our life together, especially through the years of active ministry. Most of those moves were to distant cities or places where we knew few people. It was always quite a long process getting established in a new location. Besides finding a place to live, there was the matter of getting acquainted with the area. Where are the stores and shopping places? Which roads end in a dead-end? What is the best way to get from here to there? What grocery stores carry the nicest produce and have the best prices? Who is the most reliable auto mechanic?

---

[13] See 1 Corinthians 10:31

That last question is no small item. Who can you trust? What shop will do the job right, but still not charge an exorbitant price for parts and labor? I don't begrudge someone a fair wage. Even Jesus taught that the worker deserves his wages (Luke 10:7), and Moses in his parting instructions to ancient Israel said, "Do not muzzle an ox while it is treading out the grain" (Deuteronomy 25:4). Both teach the same principle. No, I don't mind paying a good auto mechanic well, but there are two things I want to know.

First, can I depend on him (or her) for fairness and complete honesty in assessing the repairs or service my vehicle needs? In other words, does this person have a sterling character? Is he someone who always keeps his promises and is completely transparent with costs and projections? It is important to know these things!

Second, can I trust that the work done in this shop will be done right? I want to know for sure when I drive out onto the road I won't have a breakdown or accident due to faulty workmanship. I want to know the worker is truly competent before they put a wrench to my car.

Dependability is the second component of integrity. Dependability is the product of Character and Competence.

Both are necessary.

When I'm teaching on this subject I often ask the audience, "Would you prefer a mechanic who is a super nice guy with an honest heart yet lacks competence, or would you want a highly skilled technician who might tell that you need a lot of unnecessary repairs on your vehicle?

The answer, of course, is neither. We need people who are both *competent* and have impeccable *characters*.

Character means that your word is your bond. People can believe what you tell them without fail.

Competence results from initial hands-on preparation followed by continuing education.

These two factors hold regardless of your field of study or area of expertise. You can apply them to your life right now whatever your occupation or vocation. Proverbs 22:29 says, "Do you see a man who excels in his work? He will stand before kings."

To strive for excellence enhances dependability and upholds integrity.

Faithfulness

The third face of integrity is *faithfulness*.

Joseph did not endure the pit, Potiphar's house, and prison, because he knew he would end up in Pharaoh's palace. He simply remained faithful wherever he found himself. God did the rest.[14]

When my fiancée and I stood before our friend and minister on June 8, 1967, he asked both of us individually if we would be faithful to each other "so long as you both shall live." We both promised, "I will." By the grace of God our vows have remained intact for over five decades! We can categorically say: Faithfulness has its rewards!

Our love has grown richer, stronger, deeper with every passing year. Every year brings new dimensions to our relationship we could never have imagined before. Our happiness and contentment continue to grow ever more beautiful. I'm not exaggerating. Just ask her!

Faithfulness is the key.

Faithfulness encompasses respect, devotion, patience, kindness, thoughtfulness, and courtesy. They all play a part, and they all pay rich dividends. "Be faithful, even to the point of death, and I will give you the crown of life" is a promise from Jesus to the church in Smyrna (Revelation 2:10). That promise is as valid and reliable for you and me today, just as it was for believers living in the 1st century A.D.

---

[14] Attributed to H. B. Charles, Jr. (To read the story of Joseph, see Genesis 39ff.)

But, to what or to whom are we to be faithful? The answer is two-fold, and is found in Jesus' response to a question asked of him, "Which is the greatest commandment in the law?"

Jesus replied, "'Love the Lord your God with all your heart and with all your soul and with all your mind.' This is the first and greatest commandment. And the second is like it: 'Love your neighbor as yourself'" (Matthew 22:36-39).

There you have it.

Love God supremely, and your neighbor as yourself. If you love someone you will be faithful. It all stems from love—that is *agápe* love. Unconditional, unbroken, love as a principle. Love is a choice.

I have often been asked to tell a story to the children in a worship service. Several times I have taken a bill out of my wallet, and showing it to the kids I'll ask, "I want to give this money to God. How can I do that?"

Then I'll toss the bill into the air, saying, "If God is up in heaven, do you think I can just throw it up there so he can have it? How many of you think that would work?"

Of course, everybody can see how silly that is—even the adults who are listening in on this conversation!

No hands go up.

"Well," I'll say, "if that won't work, how can I get this money to God so he can use it?"

We ponder that for a few moments. Then I offer a suggestion.

"I know," I say. "Jesus told us, 'Whatever you [do] for one of the least of these brothers of mine, you did [to] me' (Matthew 25:40). So, that sounds to me that if we want to give this money to God, we can do that by doing something nice for someone in need. Maybe buying a sandwich for someone who is hungry or giving a warm coat to a cold person. What do you think? Does that sound like a good way to give this money to God?"

All the children nod in understanding. Their eyes shine with excitement as they head back to rejoin their family.

The only way to serve God, i.e. "be faithful to him," is to serve the needs of people around us. We need to learn to see the needs and learn the skills of appropriate responses. A great example is Jesus' story of the Good Samaritan.[15]

Perhaps we need to study this parable more in-depth so we can absorb its focus and principles into our daily relationships with the people of our time.

---

[15] See Luke 10:25-37

A few years ago, I got the idea I would like to have a personal motto for my life. You probably have seen those clan mottoes displayed prominently on European family crests from the Middle Ages. That was the kind of short, pithy statement I wanted—not so much for my family as for myself. Something concise, powerful, and easily remembered. A catchphrase to live by.

I found a few examples I liked, but which were not exactly what I was looking for.

A Deo et rege - "For God and King."

Dant vires gloriam - "Strength gives glory."

Facta non-verba - "Deeds not words."

I finally decided I would just have to write my own. Anyway, I thought, that would make it more authentic.

I'm enough of a traditionalist that I knew I wanted my motto to be in Latin—even though I had completely failed Latin class in high school! I had absorbed enough of the language, however, to know some basic words and grammar. Writing this simple motto shouldn't be too hard.

Hmmmmm . . . .

It wasn't the language issue that pulled me up short. I suddenly came face to face with several questions about my life.

Who am I, really?

What am I about?

How do I want to live?

What is my life's purpose?

I had to stop and seriously think through the answers to these and other similar questions. The exercise of writing this motto was like imagining what you would like to have engraved as an epitaph on your grave marker. What short statement would you like for summarizing your entire life and have it engraved in stone for anyone and everyone to read forever after you are gone?

After several years and several attempts, I finally arrived at my permanent motto. Here it is:

Vivere cum integritas en gracia dei" "To live with integrity by the grace of God."

Yes, I'd like to have that motto carved into the marker of my final earthly resting place. But, more importantly, by the grace of God I pray that I might live that motto every day until I die.

That's why the third prayer of *My Seven Essential Daily Prayers* is "Integrity in My Life."

Without integrity, nothing else matters.

How can this be achieved? Only through the power of the Holy Spirit living in and through us, and claiming the promise expressed by the Apostle

Paul, "I can do everything through him who gives me strength" (Philippians 4:13).

Study Guide

Chapter Three "Integrity in My Life"

Personal Integrity Confirms the Authenticity of our Words and Actions

1. How much transparency is needed for true integrity in your life?

2. If you have ever been "hoodwinked" by a dishonest person, what was your emotional reaction? What action did you take—if any? How might you react differently today?

3. What steps can you take to improve your competency in work or other

responsibilities? Have you already begun that journey? If not, when will you start?

4. Jesus told us to love our "neighbor" as ourselves. What does this mean to you? Whom do you consider to be your "neighbor?"

5. Try the exercise of creating a personal life-motto. You might want to journal your experience.

Your Thoughts:

_____

_____

_____

_____

_____

_____

_____

_____

Chapter Four

Joy in My Spirit

That I May Face Each Day with Strength

The joy of the Lord is your strength![16]

Retirement centers—aka "rest homes," "senior care facilities" (and other euphemistic labels used for such places)—are not necessarily the happiest places on earth. Many, if not most of the residents suffer from aches and pains common to

---

[16] Read the wonderful account which gave rise to this expression of celebration in Nehemiah 8.

advancing age. They often struggle with dimming eyesight, loss of hearing, fading strength, and other devastating health challenges. Sometimes, but not always, care staff are short-handed and overworked. Delayed attention to pressing needs can be frustrating for an old person dealing with serious pain—or in a panic to use the bathroom! It's no wonder that "happy warriors" are few and far between in many of these facilities.

But then, there was Clarissa Archer.[17]

Clarissa always had a beautiful smile on her face. She simply glowed with peace and happiness. Not that she had escaped the difficulties and trials coming from 80+ years of life. But, despite all that, Clarissa was like a bright ray of sunshine everywhere she showed up.

That wasn't always the case. At times in the past she grumbled and complained loudly about her old-age infirmities and inconveniences. She didn't like being old, and she didn't mind letting everyone around her know it. The "golden years" were *not* good, and she wasn't shy complaining about the way things were.

But then, one day all that changed.

---

[17] "Clarissa Archer" is not her real name. However, this story is based on a true account of a very real lady living in a very real situation. I was her pastor for several years.

Clarissa's son often came to take his mother into town for shopping and a sit-down restaurant meal. On this day he parked near the front door as usual and helped her into the car. After she was buckled in, Clarissa waited for her son to walk to the other side of the car and get into the driver's seat. In those few moments, she pulled the sun visor down to see the mirror on the backside. She sat gazing at her reflection as her son fastened his seatbelt and started the engine. A look of genuine concern crossed her face.

"I don't look happy," she said. "Christians are supposed to be happy. I'm going to practice being happy!"

It was more of a proclamation than a statement. Her voice carried the determination of a person making a much-needed and long-contemplated life adjustment. There was no mistaking her resolve. She was totally serious.

And she stuck to it!

That day marked the beginning of the last chapter in this precious lady's earthly life. From that time on, Clarissa could not be

> **IMPORTANT**:
> There is a genuine medical condition called "clinical depression." This may result from a variety of causes such as tumors, a chemical imbalance, or something else. Clinical depression cannot be "fixed" by just "choosing" to be happy. It is a serious issue which needs diagnosis and treatment by a qualified medical practitioner. If you think you or someone you know may be suffering from clinical depression, help is available. Don't neglect it. Talk to your doctor

seen without a smile on her face. Even now, many years after her death, the people who knew her still remember her as "the lady who was always smiling, always happy."

What an incredible testimony!

What was Clarissa's secret? She *chose* to be happy. That's right. Clarissa discovered that happiness is a choice we make regardless of the circumstances in our life. Simply put, we can choose to be happy, even in the middle of a miserable mess.

Under normal circumstances—even unpleasant ones—we have a freewill choice. We can choose to be happy. Or, we can choose to be angry, upset, resentful, bitter, or any number of similar negative emotions.

A long time ago I went through an extremely difficult experience in my ministerial career. One night, without any advance warning, and while I was present—even "chairing" a church board meeting—the members present voted unanimously to remove me from office and, effective immediately, request a replacement pastor from our denominational headquarters. To say I was devastated would be a major understatement!

I went home after that meeting shocked, confused, and bewildered. What seemed like a million questions swirled through my mind like some kind of bizarre tornado descending from a clear, blue sky. *What just happened? What's going to happen next? What about my family? How am I going to support them? What will my wife and children think? Was I ever really called to ministry? Was my pastoral service that bad? Why? Why? Why?*

I was hurt and angry. But, in my heart I knew I had to put the needs of the church first. The church needed healing, and I knew for sure that I was not the person who could bring it. With a heavy heart I called my ministerial director.

I explained what had happened, then I heard myself saying words I never dreamed I would ever say.

"This congregation is badly damaged. For some reason I'm not sure I even understand, my presence here is causing more unrest and division. It's not getting better at all. It gets worse with every week that goes by. The best thing that needs to happen here is for me to resign so you can bring another pastor to this church who can be a healer."

The next morning at about 9:30 a.m. my phone rang. It was the conference president.

"How long does it take you to drive to the office?" he asked.

"About three and a half hours," I answered.

"Good," he said. "I'll see you in here at one o'clock this afternoon."

The trip to headquarters was uneventful. My wife and I arrived promptly at the appointed time. The visit was cordial but final. About an hour later I was out of a job. I did not return to pastoral ministry for nearly three years.

The immediate aftermath of that disaster brought a flurry of transition events, moving to a different house, making major decisions for our family, getting our various affairs in order for whatever lay ahead. Every day brought new unforeseen challenges. In the middle of all that frenzy I remember intentionally making a bedrock decision.

I choose to forgive! I told myself in an internal conversation. *Bitterness is a poison that a person drinks hoping his enemy will die. I will not go down that road. I will not allow this experience to destroy me, my family, or my ministry. I have no idea what the future holds just now, but I will go there free from anger or resentment. I forgive those who caused this to happen. I forgive. I choose to be happy.*

A choice. The right choice.

From that moment until the very day as I write these words, I have seen God's hand leading me in countless uncharted paths of blessing. I can truly say with King David, "You have turned my mourning into dancing; you have put off my sackcloth and clothed me with gladness" (Psalm 30:11 NKJV). There are times when I think I need to thank those who moved against me that dark night. Without that action I would have missed the abundance of blessings I have received since then.

To be completely transparent, however, I must also confess that periodically I have to revisit my original choice of forgiveness. The Lord gives me ample opportunities to reaffirm my commitment to full forgiveness and its subsequent children happiness and joy. Satan would love to recapture that hurt and grow the fruit of bitterness in my spirit. By God's continuing grace, I cannot—will not—allow that to happen.

Many years ago, I came to realize that regardless of how many or how bad negative events might be which unfold around you, if you turn them over to God he can, and does, redeem them for good.

"Rejoice in the Lord always. I will say it again: Rejoice! (Philippians 4:4).

So, mark this down:

When we choose happiness, God gives us joy.

Joy is a gift from God. He sends it with the Holy Spirit taking up residence in the believer's heart. "The fruit of the Spirit is love, joy, peace, patience, kindness, goodness, faithfulness, gentleness, and self-control. Against such things there is no law" (Galatians 5:22, 23).

The Holy Spirit's presence is a gift directly from Jesus to believers everywhere. He promised his disciples, "The Counselor, the Holy Spirit, whom the Father will send in my name, will teach you all things and will remind you of everything I have said to you" (John 14:26).

Choosing happiness in the face of hardship, persecution, or misfortune is choosing to follow the whisperings of the Holy Spirit in your mind. I'm not saying we should pretend that bad things and bad experiences don't exist. They do, and no one enjoys them, but we don't need to be mentally and spiritually destroyed by evil events. We can choose to overcome them. We can choose to survive. We can choose forgiveness and personal happiness. The choice is always ours.

Even so, we never lose the freedom to choose the other way if we decide we want to go in that direction.

Remember the story Jesus told about the kid who left home for adventure and finally came to his senses in a pigpen?[18] When he arrived back home everybody exploded into a great celebration. Dad was ecstatic. The servants killed the fatted calf. The band played. The whole family danced and partied into the night. The lost boy was home! Joy reigned in everybody's heart!

---

[18] See Luke 15:11ff. Also Chapter Two, "Righteousness in My Heart" in this book.

Everybody, that is, except the kid's big brother. When he found out what was going on he blew up and refused to even go inside. His dad came out to try reasoning with his older son, but he would have none of it.

"Look!" he snapped, "All these years I've been slaving for you and never disobeyed your orders. Yet you never gave me even a young goat so I could celebrate with my friends. But when this son of yours who has squandered your property with prostitutes comes home, you kill the fatted calf for him!"

"My son," the father said, "you are always with me, and everything I have is yours. But we had to celebrate and be glad, because this brother of yours was dead and is alive again; he was lost and is found" (Luke 15:29-32).

Talk about a wet blanket! The kid's big brother couldn't have joy because he chose anger over happiness. His sour attitude had to have brought acute pain to his father's heart. One of his sons was lost, but alive—a cause for great rejoicing. The other cared for nothing but himself. I wonder if he saw his father's shoulders slump, or if he noticed the older man's slower, staggering steps as he turned back to the party in the house.

It is worth noting that in Luke 15 the only person without joy is the older brother. Everyone else is celebrating something lost but found. A coin. A sheep. A son. The only one who doesn't celebrate in these stories is this self-centered grown-up man-child who chooses hurt feelings over forgiveness, resentment over reason. He could have chosen love for his brother. He chose hatred instead. The fruit was hurt and heartache. The party lights shined a little dimmer for the grand occasion.

But that's what happens when we don't choose happiness. It not only blocks our joy it also steals the wind from the wings of family and friends.

Near the end of the 5th century B.C. many Jews were allowed to return to Jerusalem from exile in Babylon. The city lay in ruins from the attacks of Nebuchadnezzar's army 70 years earlier. The protective wall was destroyed. All that remained were heaps of rubble scattered chaotically around the once-thriving center of Israel's glory days. The splendor of Solomon's once-upon-a-time magnificent empire had been reduced to dust and ashes by Babylonian soldiers. Centuries of Israel's and Judah's feckless kings and faithless priests bore the fruit of neglected holiness. The scene of ruined walls and burned-out buildings was enough to make even the stoutest heart tremble.

Political winds had shifted dramatically in the seventy years of exile. The Babylonians had fallen to the power of the Medes and Persians. The Persian King Artaxerxes I now sat on the throne of the new empire. History indicates that Artaxerxes I ruled with a tolerant hand, allowing for conquered peoples to retain and practice their local traditional religions and customs. He was sympathetic to the needs of the Jews, permitting them to return to their homeland, and even authorizing the rebuilding of Jerusalem and its surrounding wall.

Artaxerxes appointed his personal cupbearer, a Jew named Nehemiah as governor of Jerusalem. Nehemiah and a priest named Ezra led the overwhelming task of reestablishing the city and reconstructing the wall.

Beyond the physical structures, they also had to lay the philosophical and religious foundations for an entirely new populace. At least two, maybe three generations had come and gone during the seven decades of exile. The vast majority of the returned exiles had never seen their ancestral homeland. Living as a "chosen people" representing the Living God was strangely unfamiliar to them. They knew little or nothing of the culture, rituals, or fundamentals of their religious heritage. Growing up under the influence of pagan Persian beliefs and practices, they needed a comprehensive crash course in how they were supposed to live, the temple services, and what it all meant for them as individuals and as a distinct people.

A day was set for a great assembly. A speaking platform was built for the occasion. In the morning of the appointed day, Ezra the priest stood on the platform and read to the people all the words of the Law of Moses—what we now call the "Pentateuch," the first five books of our Bible: Genesis, Exodus, Leviticus, Numbers, and Deuteronomy. It took a long time to read it all. And it was heavy stuff. When the people heard what Ezra was reading, they broke down and wept.

> *And Nehemiah, who was the governor, Ezra the priest and scribe, and the Levites who taught the people said to all the people, "This day is holy to the Lord your God; do not mourn nor weep." For all the people wept, when they heard the words of the Law.*

> *Then he said to them, "Go your way, eat the fat, drink the sweet, and send portions to those for whom nothing is prepared.; for this day is holy to our Lord. Do not sorrow, for the joy of the Lord is your strength"* (Nehemiah 8:9, 10 NKJV).

The joy of the Lord is your strength!

Notice this: it is the "*joy of the Lord*" that gives you strength. In other words, it is the *joy in the Lord's heart*—because of his love for you— which becomes *your* strength when his Spirit lives in you.

"The kingdom of God is . . . righteousness, peace, and joy in the Holy Spirit" (Romans 14:17).

"Rejoice in the Lord always. I will say it again: Rejoice! (Philippians 4:4).

To summarize this chapter on my fourth essential daily prayer, here are a few suggestions for keeping your heart open and growing in the "joy of the Lord:"

1. Practice (choose) an attitude of gratitude!

2. Choose happiness. Choose to forgive anyone who has wronged you. Reject the temptation to indulge in a victimhood mentality.

3. Look for things to celebrate, like beauty in nature, gracious acts of kindness by other people, Bible promises, or the gifts of life, health, and understanding.

4. Focus on the positive things of life. Set a time every day for personal Bible reading, memorization, reflection, and meditation. Accentuate the positive. Eliminate the negative.

5. There is power in praise! Psalm 22:3 says, "[God is] enthroned in the praises of Israel (NKJV). The KJV says that God *dwells* in our praise. What that teaches me is that if we want to experience God's power, we should express more of our praise to him. If God is present in our praises, so is his power. Power for joy comes from living a life of praise.

With your indulgence, I'll close this chapter with another little story.

In the early 1980's I was pastor of a small country church near Spokane, Washington. My family and I lived in a little house about two miles from the church. We had a menagerie of pets, including some horses, chickens, and goats. The children thrived on the freedom of country living and caring for their animals. It was a good life.

I owned a 1969 Ford F-250 pickup truck which I used to haul feed and firewood, tow our horse trailer, and transport other bulky items. The truck needed some service, so one morning I drove into town to an automotive shop. Ruth picked me up in our car and would bring me back when the truck was ready. Several hours later the mechanic called saying the work was done. We headed to town again. She dropped me off at the shop and left to care for some other errands she needed to run.

I stepped to the counter and the mechanic handed me the bill. I couldn't believe my eyes when I saw the bottom line! It was far more than I expected. Beyond reason!

When I objected (rather vigorously) he simply replied in somewhat of a snippy voice, "Well, we're not a discount shop here."

I was livid. There was nothing I could do but write the check, collect my keys, and head for home. I don't know when I've been so upset. Money was tight already without being severely overcharged for a couple of simple service items for my truck! It just wasn't right!

But then, on the way home, the Lord started whispering his grace in my ear. This time his grace challenged my angry attitude.

"Okay Lord," I said, "I know what I'm feeling right now is not what you would be feeling if this happened to you. Please take my angry spirit away and replace it with your joy and peace."

I began to sing . . .

Praise God from whom all blessings flow.

Praise him all creatures here below.

Praise him above ye heavenly hosts.

Praise Father, Son, and Holy Ghost!

The first time singing this doxology as I stormed along on the winding country road toward home, my voice was angry and filled with resentment. I yelled and growled the words, spitting them out through clenched teeth and a rigid jaw.

I sang the short hymn again.

The second time through I began to feel calmer and less upset. The third time I began to feel his peace. The fourth time I sang for joy!

The joy of the Lord is your strength.

The firewall you build every morning for your spiritual survival will be fortified with God's power when you find your joy in him, and his joy in you.

There is victory in Jesus!

Study Guide

Chapter Four
"Joy in My Spirit"

When We Choose Happiness and Forgiveness, God Blesses Us with Joy

1. What are five things for which you are truly grateful right now? Share with your group or write them into your journal.

2. Who in your life—past or present—might you need to forgive? Is reconciliation possible? Even if

reconciliation is NOT possible, how can you discover God's grace to forgive as He forgave you?

3. How is choosing real happiness not just a glossing-over of real problems?

4. Try writing a personal psalm of praise to God, including a tune and lyrics. You don't need to share it. It doesn't have to be great music or great poetry. It is just between you and your God.

Your Thoughts:

_____

_____

_____

_____

_____

_____

Chapter Five

Strength for My Body

That My Physical Well-being will Testify of God's Grace

Dear friend, I pray that you may enjoy good health and that all may go well with you, even as your soul is getting along well (3 John 2).

Those who wait on the Lord shall renew their strength; they shall mount up with wings like eagles, they shall run and not be weary, they shall walk and not faint (Isaiah 40:31 NKJV).

If the Spirit of him who raised Jesus from the dead dwells in you, he who raised Christ from the dead will also give life to your mortal bodies through his Spirit who dwells in you (Romans 8:11).

An unavoidable, inconvenient truth: Time marches on. We're all going to die. Bummer, isn't it?

But, here is a question: What kind of legacy will we leave behind?

My childhood physician, Dr. Frank Shearer lived for 107 years. When National Geographic Magazine ran an article featuring regions of the world where large percentages of the population live past 100 years—places known as "Blue Zones"—Dr. Frank's picture appeared with him on water skis at age one-hundred-and-one! That was in September 2005. I was excited to see someone from my "world" show up in that prestigious journal. Quite a few years before that, our paths had crossed at a cowboy campmeeting where I discovered he was an avid horseman, something I didn't know previously. I hadn't seen him in nearly 30 years since I was a child. He was about 94 or 95 then.

Dr. Frank's entire life was adventure, discovery, and generosity. In 1925 he began practicing medicine in the tiny agricultural community of Toppenish, Washington. During the Great Depression years of the 1930s, payment for his services often came in the form of fruit, vegetables, or a chicken. He did house calls and never refused service to anyone for a lack of funds. Besides his patients—and those horses—he also loved water sports, fishing, hunting, and hiking the trails of the great Pacific Northwest. Through the years he owned several airplanes and loved to fly when he was called upon to travel. He lived his life to serve and encourage others. Dr. Frank Shearer was an incredible human being. I have only recently grown to appreciate the privilege and honor it was to be one of his many patients.

How did he do it? What kind of spirit drives a man to live that long with his never-ending passion for life? What wellspring provides such a fountain of vibrant longevity? Is it something all the rest of us can find, as well?

I love the story told at former President George H. W. Bush's funeral that he once said, "The goal is to die young as old as possible!" President Bush was 94 when he died. He kept his upbeat attitude to the very end. What a great example for us all.

Sadly, we've all heard stories about people who retire, get bored, and soon die just sitting in the easy chair. Who wants to end up like that? No one! Certainly not me. And, I suspect, not you either.

Every day is a new day with God. *My Seven Essential Daily Prayers* have been revolutionary for my walk with the Creator/Redeemer/King. That's why I have felt so called to share them with everyone I can. I covet this rich spiritual walk for every person reading this book. I hope the idea of these priority prayers will impact your life as profoundly as they have mine.

The focus of prayer in this chapter is "Strength for My Body." I'm going to spend the bulk of the time here talking about the amazing machine that God has designed for our earthly residence. But before we begin there are two things I need to put up front.

First, even though I'll be covering a lot of detail with general information about the human body and healthful living practices, the core message here is our relationship to the Creator, his purpose for giving us life, and our part in keeping mind and body in good working order.

Second, I am neither an expert nor an authority in the arenas of physical health and wellbeing. I can't—and don't—claim any advanced training in these areas. The closest I come to that is getting an undergraduate academic minor in HPE&R (Health, Physical Education, and Recreation) once-upon-a-time in the long, long ago. Nevertheless, it is well known that the health of our bodies bears a direct relationship to both mental and spiritual wellness. Both suffer when our body is sick, weak, or exhausted. To find optimal strength mentally and spiritually, we need to treat the body the best we can for the best health we can achieve. The material in this chapter is presented with that idea in mind.

I heard a funny story several years ago. It seems a fellow was hiking in the Appalachian Mountains when he noticed a lot of smoke curling into the sky above a ridge just ahead. He ran up the trail to find the fire. As he rounded a corner and came over the summit, he saw a cabin with the back porch nearly engulfed in flames. He rushed to see what he might do to help. When he got closer, he saw an old mountain man sitting on the front porch leaning back in his rocking chair casually smoking a corncob pipe.

"Hey!" the hiker yelled. "Your house is on fire!"

The old-timer looked up, slowly took another puff on his pipe, and drawled, "Yeah, I know. I been sittin' here prayin' about that!"

Okay. Now that you've probably chuckled at that little tale, let's apply it to real life. Praying is good. We should always pray about all our troubles. But many times—especially in the arenas of health and wellness—the answers we get are directly related to our choice of actions. Putting healthy habits to work with our prayers will generally get more desirable results than simply praying and not acting. It's just the way things are.

Here's a simple concept: *We are **stewards** of God's gifts of life, health, and strength.* A steward is a caretaker of someone else's belongings.

Imagine a medieval estate. Somewhere on the property stands a great house or maybe a castle. That is the home of the "Lord of the Manor" and his immediate family. It would typically be staffed with many household servants charged with various responsibilities like cleaning, cooking, serving meals, laundry, and whatever else needed attention. At a distance from the manor would be various carriage houses, barns, sheds, etc. There would be pens and shelters for keeping animals—horses, cows, sheep, pigs, etc. The buildings might even include living quarters for the hired servants who cared for this part of the lord's enterprises.

In Middle-English a pen for the animals was called a "sty" as in "pigsty." The word was used for the pens of other animals as well as pigs. The hired servant in charge of the sty and the animals it held was called a "sty-warden." Now, centuries later, those two words have fused to give us our current word "steward."

The "sty-warden" aka "steward" did not own the animals himself. He was only charged with their care. He was accountable to his employer, the Lord of the Manor, who was the actual owner.

In our case, God is the ultimate Owner of Everything, including the very body housing our individual life here on Earth. He has both created us and redeemed us, so we are twice his. People who say, "It's my body. I can do with it what I please," totally miss the mark. If we accept the premise that even our body is designed and created by God, and that he lovingly provides it for our earthly existence, then it all belongs to him.

We are stewards of this magnificent gift. He gives us the freedom to do as we will with it, but if we recognize and accept that everything we are and have ultimately belongs to him, and if we love and respect him as Lord of Everything, we will make every sincere effort to honor him with our entire self—body, mind, and spirit.

King David of Ancient Israel understood the incredible wonder of the human body. In one of his most beautiful song-poems he wrote, "I praise you because I am fearfully and wonderfully made; your works are wonderful, I know full well" (Psalm 139:14).

Let's take a quick look at a few of the fully integrated, synchronized systems built into our body.

Musculoskeletal System:

There is a fun story told by the Old Testament prophet Ezekiel about his vision of an entire valley filled with hundreds of dry bones[19]. The Lord tells Ezekiel to prophesy to the bones so that he (God) can restore the life of all those dead soldiers. Ezekiel does as he is told, then writes, "there was a

---

[19] Read the story in Ezekiel 37:1-14.

noise, and suddenly a rattling; and the bones came together, bone to bone" (Ezekiel 37:7 NKJV).

Imagine the action! *Clackety-clack, rattle, rattle, snap, crackle, pop, pop, pop!* That must have made Ezekiel's hair stand on end! And, it must have gone on for quite a while, too.

All those dry bones assembled themselves into bare skeletons. Sinews, muscles, and tendons began covering the bones, and finally, skin provided the outside layer of each body. The Lord then tells Ezekiel to command the breath of life to come from the four winds of heaven, saying, "Come from the four winds, O breath, and breathe into these slain, that they may live" (verse 9). Ezekiel prophesies again and the corpses come to life and stand to their feet, a great army!

(If you're like me, about now you have that old Negro spiritual playing in your head, "Dem bones, dem bones, dem dry bones . . . Now hear the word of the Lord!")

The lesson, God tells Ezekiel, is for the people of Israel, that he—Yahweh—can, and will, restore life to their destroyed nation, and by this they will know that he reigns in power and majesty.

It seems like a great message for us, too. God both gives and sustains life. He is the Source and Foundation of our existence.

With that, let's look a little closer at our own not-so-dry bones.

An adult human body normally has 206 bones, each with a specialized function. Most of us rarely think consciously about our bones. With a closer examination, however, we discover that these organs which provide the basic platform of our physical existence are far more complex than simple foundation parts supporting the rest of body functions.

- The long bones of the legs and arms, the pelvis, ribs, sternum, and vertebrae are hollow, containing marrow for producing blood cells.

- The tiny bones in the ear—the hammer, anvil, and stirrup—enable hearing by converting sound vibrations in the air into electrical signals for the aural nerve to carry to the hearing center of our brain.

- Each hand is composed of twenty-seven (27!) bones perfectly arranged to articulate incredibly complex motions, giving humans quantum superiority over all other creatures on earth to develop unique cultural expressions.

On top of and attached to the bones are muscles and tendons arranged in a masterful, functional order. Flexors and extensors move the limbs, control posture, keep the body composed and stabilized, and enable us to walk upright on two legs. Tough, strap-like tendons from the muscles attach to their partner bones in strategic locations so when the muscle contracts the bones move.

Depending on how the muscles are counted, there are somewhere between 640-850 of them in your body. Some muscles like the heart and intestines have other, specialized functions, but every single muscle is there for a purpose.

The marvelous Musculoskeletal System is beyond amazing.

Respiratory System:

Breathing is pretty basic. A person may live several weeks without food, perhaps a few days without water, but only a matter of minutes without air. Immediately after being born the very first thing a baby must do is start breathing. At the end of life—whenever it comes—we often refer to that last moment as, "He drew his last breath."

Although the number of in-and-out breaths per minute while resting varies significantly from infants to adults, a general average of around 12 will work for us here. Do the math: 12 breaths/minute x 60 minutes=720 breaths in an hour, 17,280 breaths per 24 hours, 6,307,200 breaths a year, and over 441.5 million breaths in a lifetime of 70 years! Along the way, we might experience colds, touches of flu, pneumonia, cancer, toxic fumes, overheated rooms, or freezing temps, but so long as life lasts our lungs and related equipment just keep working away non-stop, night and day, day in and day out, asleep or awake. It boggles the mind.

The breathing "equipment" itself is impressive.

- Two lungs reside in the chest near the spine. The right lung has three lobes and is slightly larger than the left which shares space with the heart and accommodates that need by having only two lobes instead of three. Together the two lungs weigh (on average) close to three pounds.

- The lungs have a concave (inwardly curved) lower surface which sits on the domed diaphragm muscle separating the chest from the abdomen. As the diaphragm pulls downward it expands the lungs, drawing air through the breathing passageways into the interior. This is the action that continuously repeats automatically night and day, keeping us alive even when we are asleep or unconscious.

- Within the lungs the air passageways divide into smaller and smaller tubes and tubules until they reach the microscopic level where tiny balloon-shaped "alveoli" wait to work their magic. The total distance of all airways added together is more than 1,200 miles, with 300-500 *million* alveoli at the ends of those channels.

- Alveoli are the working "boots on the ground" soldiers of respiration. Incoming air is rich in oxygen which body cells need for oxidizing nutritional fuel into useful energy. Alveoli grab oxygen molecules from inhaled air and transfer them to red cell carriers in the bloodstream, which in turn deliver those same oxygen molecules to their destination cells. The red blood cells then pick up discarded carbon dioxide cells, transport them back to the lungs, and deliver them to the alveoli which release them into the air for exhalation. All of this process, of course, takes place a matter of mere seconds. While you are reading this, consciously take in a deep breath and immediately exhale. That's the speed of these transfers. Oxygen in. CO_2 out. Over and over. Every time you breathe. Over 6.3 million times a year.

Methinks we should really be kind to these tiny "foot-soldiers" for all they do to keep us healthy and happy. They deserve our respect and support.

Circulatory System:

Sometime during my seventh-grade year, our school showed a new hour-long "made for TV" film named "Hemo the Magnificent."[20] This mixed

---

[20] To watch "Hemo the Magnificent" on YouTube, go to **https://www.youtube.com** and do a search for the film title.

animation/live-action movie illustrated complex scientific workings of the heart, lungs, arteries, and veins carrying blood throughout the body. It featured the role of hemoglobin—aka "Hemo" in the story—carrying oxygen from the lungs out to the body and bringing CO_2 back for disposal. Bear in mind, this movie was made over 60 years ago in 1957, but even now still it masterfully portrays the inner workings of the circulatory system so even young children can understand it.

The "heart" of the system is the heart muscle itself. *Lub-dub, lub-dub, lub-dub,* this four-chambered living pump repeats itself over and over, resting only momentarily between every beat. Barring disease, accident, or other unfortunate incidents, this miracle muscle continues without interruption for a lifetime of service to the body.

Science has vastly expanded its knowledge of the heart in the last six decades. Today, open heart surgeries, valve replacements, multiple by-pass operations, even complete heart transplants are common. Those medical procedures were unimaginable when "Hemo" first appeared on the screen.

The purpose of the heart pump and the entire circulation system is to supply oxygen and nutrient-rich blood to the body and carry away impurities and waste. Without blood flowing through the vessels death quickly arrives. I know from personal experience how dangerous a significant loss of blood can be. Twice in my lifetime I have come close to bleeding out. Only miracles preserved my life on each occurrence.

When I was 11 years old, I was severely injured in an accident with my American Saddlebred mare. We tumbled backward over the side of a small bridge when she reared in fear. My body was crushed against the ends of two rusty bolts as we fell onto a large wooden water pipe used for irrigation. Those two bolts punctured my left side, broke a rib, and punctured a lung. If it had not been for a neighbor girl, Janet Mason, I would never have survived. She just "happened" to see the accident, and her quick action saved my life. The black stains of my blood stayed on those bolts for many years until the old wooden pipe was replaced by a new one made of stainless steel. I very well could have "bled out" right there on the spot, but by the grace of God and Janet's quick thinking, I lived to see many more days. As you can well imagine, quite a few blood transfusions were needed to restore and preserve my life.[21]

The second incident involved a bleeding GERD ulcer when I was in my early 50's. That one took 5 units and an overnight hospital stay to get me back up to speed. The miracle here was advanced medical knowledge, skilled hospital workers, and readily available supplies of blood and medicine.

---

[21] You can read this story in its entirety in my book "Whoa! I Yelled, 'Whoa!" available from *https://amazon.com/author/lorenfenton*

I've learned to take nothing for granted. Any breakdown of the system at any point could easily have spelled my doom. I am grateful and thank God for every blessing.

And my heart still carries on. *Lub-dub, lub-dub, lub-dub.*

Nervous System:

The heart and lungs are not the only organs in your body that work around the clock for you. Your brain is—quite literally—the most sophisticated, powerful computer to be found anywhere on Planet Earth. It never sleeps, even when you do! In recent decades, great strides have been made in understanding the inner workings of this small organ[22].

Take strokes, for example.

Back in the mid-1950s my mother's aunt suffered a quite-severe stroke. No one back then even came close to understanding the cause. Strokes were shrouded in deep mystery, the stuff of old wives' tales, spooky myths, and scary legends.

My great-aunt's post-stroke life was bizarre and sometimes funny. To my shame I found her antics

---

[22] On average, an adult human brain weighs only around three pounds, and is approximately six inches long.

both terrifying and entertaining. Even the very term "stroke" implied that something supernatural or evil had touched her brain and messed up her mind. I was afraid of her. The adults in her family were confused and saddened by her condition.

Today we know so much more! Causes of strokes can be blood clots, tumors, or brain trauma. Doctors now have the knowledge and ability to immediately reverse the effects if they have a timely opportunity and the right conditions. It is truly wonderful what modern medicine can do.

Have you ever had a tiny, almost invisible sliver stuck in your finger? How did you know it was there? You could feel it, of course! Every time you picked something up, or brushed your hand against a doorknob, or lifted a piece of paper, that nearly microscopic sticker reminded you that it was there, and it wasn't going away. I'd guess it may have been so irritating that you finally had to drop everything else so you could focus completely on getting it removed. Once it was gone, however, you could get back to business and forget it was ever a problem.

Here's something amazing about this little scenario. Your brain was the real center processing pain from that tiny spot on your finger, but you knew exactly—with perfect precision—where to look to find it. Trillions of nerve cells throughout your body stream unbroken statuses up to headquarters, which continuously monitors every square micro-millimeter of your person. So long as you live, the nervous super-highway never stops zinging messages to and from your brain. It's pretty much how you know you are alive.

The Creator knew you would need to know.

You're welcome.

Our wonderful bodies have many more systems working non-stop—in perfect synchronization—with those we've explored above. Nevertheless, from just the few we have looked at we can see how incredibly complex and beautiful God made this earthly house we often take so much for granted.

The Apostle Paul said, "In [God] we live and move and have our being" (Acts 17:28). God himself is the source of our strength. The Holy Spirit living in our heart energizes our physical body and gives us life. "If the Spirit of him who raised Jesus from the dead dwells in you, he who raised Christ from the dead will also give life to your mortal bodies through his Spirit who dwells in you" (Romans 8:11). Knowing this, it is entirely appropriate for one of our essential daily prayers to be "strength for my body."

I feel great assurance when I wake up every morning realizing my life is empowered by the ever-present Spirit of the living God.

Here is an important truth, however: Becoming aware of the majesty and magnificence of our being is only the first step. As God does his part, we also have a responsibility. If we are serious about *praying* for strength, the next step is to *choose life practices* that are known to provide optimal health and well-being. Remember, we are stewards—caretakers—of this inestimable gift of God's grace, our very body.

How do we do that? How do we choose the best? How do we live as faithful and responsible stewards?

Here are some suggestions:

1. Start with a good attitude (You might want to go back and read Chapter 4, "Joy in My Spirit" again.)

2. Follow a healthful lifestyle

3. Educate yourself in basic principles of healthful living

4. Avoid fads and extremes

5. Memorize and incorporate natural, common-sense practices into your daily life—like these:

Diet

Science, and an ever-growing body of testimonial evidence, suggest that a mostly plant-based food plan works best for weight control, muscle strength, energy management, mental alertness, and a host of other benefits.

One excellent source of information and documentation is the *Forks Over Knives Plan: How to Transition to the Life-Saving, Whole-Food, Plant-Based Diet* by Alona Pulde, MD, and Matthew Lederman, MD. I highly recommend that you check out their website[23].

Water

Water is the most common compound found on our planet. All life as we know it is dependent on this amazing molecule—two hydrogen atoms bonded to one of oxygen, aka "H_2O."

Human bodies average between 50-75% water, depending on age, body mass, and gender. Overweight people tend to have less body-water than more fit individuals because fat contains less water than lean muscle. Men's bodies generally have a larger percentage of water than women,

---

[23] Full information on this plan is available at **https://www.forksoverknives.com/**. (Disclaimer: I have received no compensation, material or otherwise, from this organization, or any other referenced source throughout this book. I include them here because I personally have found them helpful and beneficial.)

because women typically carry more fat than men. Babies' bodies can be up to 75% water.[24]

How much water intake should you have each day? Recent guidelines recommend *Your body weight (lbs.) divided by two*. Drink that many ounces of water every 24 hours. Example: A man weighing 150 lbs. should take in 75 ounces of fluid every day. That would be around 8-9 8oz glasses per day. With that simple formula you can do the math for your personal needs.

Exercise

I have to confess—a productive exercise program is hard for me to follow with reasonable consistency. No excuses. I just struggle with making it happen on a regular, daily basis. I am well aware that needs to change. If I am writing this in a book and recommending it to others, I need to be doing it myself, right? Exactly. Even my doctor makes a point to remind me what I should be doing every time I see him.

Not to worry, I have a plan.

I recently purchased an activity tracker—a Fitbit Charge 3. This little wrist-band device will be my "exercise-diet-sleep-weight monitor-water intake-and-calorie counter" from now until some incalculable future date when I may deem it no

---

[24] https://www.thoughtco.com/how-much-of-your-body-is-water-609406

longer necessary. Quite frankly, I am looking forward to the journey using this thing. It appears to be a good fit for giving me the extra nudge I need. The goal is 10,000-12,000 steps a day. Reaching that milestone will be a day for me to celebrate, for sure!

A word of caution: If you decide to start an exercise program, you need to first counsel with your personal health-care professional. Too many people have run into serious physical problems without realizing the danger they could bring upon themselves by starting too fast, overdoing it, and end up paying a huge, unexpected, and unwanted price. For some, the price has been sudden death. Don't let that happen to you. Talk to your doctor. First.

Why be concerned about exercise? Because it is part of being in the best health possible. It is all about the stewardship factor. It is one more way we can testify to the greatness of our awesome Creator God.

Rest/Sleep

I love a good night's sleep—and naps! I inherited my mother's ability to take a 15-20-minute nap and wake up refreshed and ready to continue whatever I was doing. Not everyone can do the power nap thing, but it sure works for me. If you can, try zoning out for a quick few minutes in the middle of your day. It may give you just the boost you need for finishing an important task.

Have you ever thought about the business side of sleep? It is huge! A quick online check reveals that current estimates (2019) indicate the annual sleep-health industry may be worth between $60-$80 *billion* dollars in the United States alone. Bedroom furniture and decor, comfortable sleepwear, soothing bath and beauty products, prescription medications, and OTC sleep aids are just a few of the many items Americans buy every day hoping to improve their sleep.

The quality of a person's waking hours is directly affected by the length and depth of recent sleep time. Productivity at work, focus at study, skill at play, recreational activities, personal relationships at home or in the office—just a few areas of everyday life that are improved by healthy, timely sleep.[25]

We all feel the need for great, restorative, healing sleep. Our culture pays out big bucks attempting to make it happen.

Getting enough sleep is vital for health, overall wellness, and productivity. So is taking a periodic rest-break during your waking hours. In his blockbuster book *The 7 Habits of Highly Effective*

---

[25] The opposite factor of fatigue is a major issue. Check out this website: https://www.nsc.org/work-safety/safety-topics/fatigue

People,[26] author Stephen R. Covey lists "Sharpening the Saw: Principles of Balanced Self-Renewal" as the one personal habit that keeps all the others functioning at optimal levels. Dr. Covey uses the illustration of cutting wood with a dull saw vs. a sharp saw. The worker who takes time away from actual cutting to keep his tool sharp is much more efficient—aka "productive"—in both the amount of wood cut and the energy needed to cut it. Granted, most of us aren't woodcutters, but the principle remains. Taking time for rest and renewal will generally increase our energy for the task at hand as well as the output of our efforts.

The same principle applies on a broader scale as well. Being raised as a Seventh-day Adventist, I was taught from my earliest days about the value of a weekly sabbath—a day of rest. At the time of Creation, God gave humanity a very special gift: the weekly Sabbath.[27] Later, the Lord even included this Sabbath gift as one of the Ten Commandments given to the Israelites through Moses on Mt. Sinai. God—our Creator—knew that human beings would work best, live longer, and be happier with a weekly routine, including an entire day when secular and business concerns could be

---

[26] Covey, Stephen R., The 7 Habits of Highly Effective People: Restoring the Character Ethic. Simon & Schuster (Fireside Book), New York, 1989.

[27] See Genesis 2:1-3; Exodus 20:8-11

set aside, allowing us to focus on personal peace, healthy relationships, and spiritual growth.

Try it! It works!

Sunshine

I think I might understand a tiny bit about why ancient cultures worshiped the sun—the most important of all gods in the pantheon of many tribes around the world. Appeasement of 'gods" and 'goddesses" to acquire benefits like food, fertility, good luck, and good health were the primary driving factor of life. Sacrificing to the "gods" was commonplace. With the sun being the foremost deity in most religious cultures, it was natural to put him—always a male deity—at the head of every list, even giving him first place in the days of the week, e.g. the "*sun's*-day." The first day of every week became a day of worship and celebration honoring the sun—and all the benefits it brings to the earth—long before the arrival of Christianity. The ancients believed that the sun made everything possible—from rains watering their fields to the growth of crops, to the abundance of game, to providing the light of day overcoming the darkness of night. In their minds the sun was to be worshiped so he would continue to bless them with what they needed.

In a way, they were right.

So far as the physical mechanics of the solar system is concerned, the sun does—in fact—make nearly everything happen here on Earth. The miracles of photosynthesis, for instance, could not occur without sunshine. Without photosynthesis there would be no green plants. Without plants there would be no food for humans or animals. There would be no fossil fuels to drive our cars, or firewood to burn in the fireplace, let alone timber with which to frame our houses. Without sunshine there would be no evaporation from the oceans, no clouds to water the land, no wind to carry the waters over the land, no rivers for hydro-electric power, or for fish to swim. In short, sunshine is the powerhouse factor driving every natural action in the world. Without sunshine, there is no life as we know it. Not even our own.

Sunshine also does marvelous things in our own body, too. For instance, sunlight with adequate amounts of UV-B radiation interacts with a type of cholesterol in our skin to produce cholecalciferol (AKA vitamin D3). Proper levels of vitamin D3 contribute to improved bone density, brain health, a stronger immune system, weight control, and lower occurrences of autoimmune diseases.[28]

If you are unsure of how much vitamin D3 you have, ask your doctor to order a blood chemistry panel for analysis. Once you have that information you can move ahead with any corrective protocol, if it may be needed. Winter sun in latitudes further from the equator does not

---

[28] A quick online search for the benefits of vitamin D3 will provide a great volume of information on this subject.

provide the UV-B rays needed for your skin to produce vitamin D3, so some supplementation may be needed. Check with your doctor.[29]

A word of caution about too much sunshine, however:

Have you ever had a seriously bad sunburn? Unfortunately, I have gone through several of those painful experiences. Never again! I mention that because exposure to too much solar radiation can do serious damage to your skin. While you need the sun on your skin for its benefits, overdoing it can harm the cells and eventually result in skin cancer. Balance and moderation is the key.

Temperance

Sometime along in my teen years our church youth leaders handed out a "Temperance Pledge" and encouraged all of us to sign it so we could then carry it with us as a ready reminder of our commitment to sobriety and healthful living. Along with all the other young people, I gladly and willingly signed the pledge. I had the little card in my wallet for many years, until somewhere along the way it disappeared. But I didn't need it in my pocket. The message was written deep in my heart.

---

29 Here is a link to a YouTube video showing how to find the levels of UV-B at your location at any given day of the year: **https://youtu.be/vS9acVgQjZY**

Part of my family heritage is anything but pretty. In the very early 20th century my father's family moved from Missouri/Kansas to northern Idaho for work in the silver-lead ore mines. Orofino was a rough town, filled with hardscrabble miners and loggers. In those days, alcohol flowed like water in the saloons and bars.

After only a few short years my grandfather Arthur Fenton became a severe alcoholic. One tragic day in 1907, he ran away from his family and didn't return. It was decades before his family saw him again. My dad was 11 years old.

That one act created chaos in the Fenton family. Its echoes still rumble more than a century later.

My father and his three sisters—mere children at the time—were each "farmed out" to foster families. Grandma did the best she could but simply could not support them alone. The girls became very bitter and resentful toward their father. My father struggled with abandonment issues for years. Because of alcohol's evil effects on his family and himself, he refused to drink it in any form, ever. He cursed it until the day he died. I was never tempted to drink. I knew the generational history. I knew it wasn't good. I wanted no part of it.

Another sad spin-off of that abandonment, however, was that my father started smoking almost immediately afterward. From age 11 until he died at age 75, King Nicotine owned his lungs. Throughout my childhood and growing-up years, nearly every night a nasty smoker's cough racked my dad's body until he could clear the mucus and phlegm. Emphysema eventually took his life.

I saw the first-hand bitter fruit of smoking, up front and personal. No way did I want that for myself. So, signing the Temperance Pledge was a no-brainer for me. I had neither need nor desire to travel those roads of destruction.

Traditionally, temperance was defined as "total abstinence from that which is harmful; moderation in that which is good." But I recently made what I considered a thrilling discovery—at least for me.

The biblical Greek word *egkrateia* (pronounced "eng-kra-TIA") is rendered as "moderation" in most English translations, carrying a rather milk-toast implication of "balance," or "just a little bit is okay." However, *egkrateia* carries much more force than that!

What it really means is *true mastery from within!* Genuine *egkrateia* embodies the concepts of total self-control, self-discipline, self-mastery, and self-restraint. It could be defined as "true personal righteousness."

The trouble with this, however, is that reaching this state of personal mastery is completely impossible, even in the strength of our most resolute determinations or efforts. If *egkrateia* equates to personal righteousness—which it does—the Bible is clear: we don't have it and can't get it on our own. Isaiah 64:6 says, "All our righteous acts are like filthy rags." In other words, even the good things we attempt are all tainted with the poison of self-centeredness and sin.

Egkrateia is a spiritual fruit of God's Spirit dwelling in our heart.[30] Praying for strength for our body, then, is to pray for the Holy Spirit's gift of *true mastery from within,* enabling us to choose—and live—a healthy life of energy and vitality for the glory of God.

Fresh Air

Every time I visit a doctor for a check-up the attending nurse clips a little device to one of my fingertips. This small clip measures and reports the amount of oxygen saturation in my blood. A "sats" reading above 97% is good; less than 90% sets off alarms.

Low oxygen content can be the result of a variety of conditions, resulting in serious damage to our body. Internal organs can fail, brain function slows or ceases, and general functions become impaired or fail.

On the other hand, consider the joy of filling your lungs with a deep breath of cool fresh air after being stuck for hours in a stuffy, over-heated room!

---

[30] See Galatians 5:22-23

Wonderful, isn't it? When I was a youngster my friends and I could never decide if it "felt good," or "tasted good." I still haven't figured that one out. It was awesome whatever you called it.

There's a good reason it feels so great. The oxygen we get in the fresh air does amazing things for us. Take a low intensity walk outside after a meal. The exercise stimulates your heart and increases your circulation. Your breathing rate increases, delivering a larger volume of oxygen to the body cells.

Oxygen aids in digestion and benefits vital functions like blood pressure and heart rate. Processing oxygen helps produce serotonin—a body hormone that makes you feel happier and more content. Your white blood cells—the disease defenders—are fired by oxygen to fight and kill harmful bacteria, bolstering your immune system.

Getting adequate oxygen also helps you think more clearly, boosts your energy levels, and helps you concentrate. Breathing all that fresh air cleanses your lungs, expands the airways, and expels body toxins like carbon dioxide (CO_2).

In terms of a current slang expression, fresh air is some incredible "awesome sauce!"

Where do we get this magic mixture of breathable beneficence? Go outdoors, out of the city. Go to a park, a nature preserve, to the beach, to the mountains, or a forest. Anywhere away from smog and air pollution. If you live in a place of little pollution, open your bedroom windows at night and enjoy the refreshing night breezes.

If all this is impractical or unavailable to you, invest in an air filtering machine for your living quarters. Many brands and styles are available. They not only filter dust and other impurities, but some are also equipped to sanitize the air, making it healthier for you to breathe. The better the quality of the air around you, the better it can serve your body's health requirements.

A clear mind, clean lungs, and great energy are powerful factors for positive, praise-filled living. God's gift of fresh air for our world is a major factor making that possible.

Trust in Divine Power

One day during my sophomore year in college I opened my dorm mailbox and was delighted to see an envelope with my sister's return address printed in the corner. Opening it, I discovered a small card with this printed text: "Trust in the Lord with all your heart and lean not on your own understanding; in all your ways acknowledge him, and he shall direct your paths" (Proverbs 3:5-6 NKJV). That promise has been precious to me through all the years since then. God is good!

Can God be trusted? Absolutely. Without a doubt.

I wish I could say that my trust in God has been one unbroken journey, moving forward from faith to faith. Sadly, I cannot. There have been way too many times when I presumptively jumped ahead of his leading or turned off of the highway to heaven chasing some elusive fantasy.

Not long after I gave my heart to the Lord at age 16, I discovered a Bible promise that became a lifelong "touchstone" text for me: "Have I not commanded you? Be strong and courageous. Do not be terrified; do not be discouraged, for the Lord your God will be with you wherever you go" (Joshua 1:9). The moment I read that statement—which God made to Joshua assuring him of success in the task ahead—I knew I could also claim it as my own. I did, and the Lord has kept his side of the deal with me, just as he promised Joshua and was faithful to him in the conquest of Canaan.

I can truthfully say that even on days when I wandered off the path and turned my focus elsewhere, he never abandoned either me or his word. You can depend on God.

Trusting God's providence is better than living in fear of an unknown tomorrow.

Trusting God's love is better than fearing his punishment.

Trusting God's peace is better than fighting the storms of life without shelter.

Trusting God's presence is better than weeping in the shadows of loneliness and loss.

Trusting God's light is better than cursing the darkness.

Trusting God's strength is better than succumbing to human weaknesses of body, mind, or spirit.

Trusting God's salvation is better than dying without hope for a better tomorrow.

Trusting God is just a better way to live.

Study Guide

Chapter Five
"Strength for My Body"

Caring for our Personal Health Reveals Love and Appreciation for Our Creator Who Gives us Everything

1. What do you want to be the legacy of your life? What steps might you need to take now for that to happen? When will you begin?

2. Explore the ideas of stewardship. How many areas can you identify in which you are expected to preserve, protect, and care for things (material or otherwise) which were entrusted or bequeathed to you by someone else?

3. How long has it been since you did a healthy-living personal audit?

4. What goals will you establish in your quest for better mental, spiritual, and physical health?

5. What will be the best way for you to incorporate and habitualize the eight natural elements of health as described in this chapter?

6. What does the word "temperance" mean to you?

Your Thoughts:

_____

_____

_____

_____

_____

_____

_____

_____

_____

_____

_____

_____

_____

_____

Chapter Six

Wisdom for My Counsel

That the Fear of the Lord Might ever be My Guide

God grant me the SERENITY to accept things I cannot change; The COURAGE to change things I can, and the WISDOM to know the difference.[31]

Wisdom is better than weapons of war (Ecclesiastes 9:18).

I never had the privilege of sitting at the feet of Dr. Edward Heppenstall, one of the most influential Seventh-day Adventist theologians of the

---

[31] This "Serenity Prayer" is used in many 12-step programs such as Alcoholics Anonymous.

20th century. When I arrived at the theological seminary at Andrews University in 1998, Dr. Heppenstall had already transferred to teach for a few years at Loma Linda University before retirement. A good friend and colleague of mine did attend his classes at Andrews, however. My friend often quoted a statement he attributed to Dr. Heppenstall's lectures: He said, "The mark of a mature mind is to withhold judgment until all the facts are in."

It occurs to me that we could nicely paraphrase that statement to say, "The mark of wisdom is to get as much information as possible before jumping to conclusions."

Let's look at something Jesus said: "Behold, I send you forth as sheep in the midst of wolves: be ye therefore wise (Greek: *phrónimos*) as serpents, and harmless as doves" (Matthew 10:16 KJV). Many modern versions translate the Greek word *phrónimos* as "shrewd," as in "shrewd as serpents." A quick check of an analytical concordance shows some other possibilities. Personally, I like "prudent," "judicious," "well-advised," "sensible," and "cautious."

In other words, Jesus told his disciples to use some common sense when dealing with people who might initially appear friendly, but who are, in reality, dead set opposed to them. That sounds like "wisdom" to me.

Simon Peter's brother John echoed Jesus' teaching in his first letter to the believers, "Dear friends, do not believe every spirit, but test the spirits to see whether they are from God" (1 John 4:1).

Think, analyze, consider. Don't be naive or gullible. Get all the facts. Then, act accordingly.

The ever-analytical and always eloquent Apostle Paul made this fascinating observation: "Jews demand miraculous signs and Greeks look for wisdom, but we preach Christ crucified: a stumbling block to Jews and foolishness to Gentiles, but to those whom God has called, both Jews and Greeks, Christ the power of God and the wisdom of God" (1 Corinthians 1:22-25).

We need to take a closer look at Paul's statement.

In the Old Testament Hebrew language, the word for "wisdom" was *chokmah*. This word carried several meanings or implications. For instance, *chokmah* could mean skill in war, wisdom in administration, shrewdness, prudence in religious affairs, or insight for ethical and religious settings. The specific meaning had to be understood from the context of the surrounding text.

In the 1st century A.D. during the time of Jesus and later, the basis of Jewish acceptance of truth and wisdom was any kind of supernatural sign. The Jews repeatedly asked Jesus, "What miraculous sign can you show us to prove your authority to do all this? (John 2:18), and "What miraculous sign will you give that we may see it and believe you?

(John 6:30). These questions came both from the leaders (scribes, Pharisees, etc.) and from the common people who were schooled by the teachings of the priests.

When Jesus didn't give them such a sign, many no longer followed him. They couldn't accept a "prophet" who refused to entertain them with the "miracles" they wanted to see.

The Greeks, on the other hand—whose developing cultural timeline roughly parallels that of ancient Israel—looked for wisdom from their philosophers. The Greek philosopher-teachers were men who "loved wisdom." Our modern word "philosophy" comes from joining two Greek words *philos* (to love) and *sophia* (wisdom).

The influence of these ancient teachers continues to dominate much of our Western culture including many of the unwritten "rules" of society even to the present day.

The three most famous Greek philosophers were Socrates, Plato, and Aristotle. Following the methods of teaching pioneered by these three, the Greeks evolved an entire society dedicated to the discovery of truth through philosophical debate, discussion, and constant exploration of ideas. The Apostle Paul encountered this in his visit to Athens when he met with some of these scholars on Mars Hill.

The Greek people built magnificent temples to their gods and goddesses. In mid-fifth century

B.C. the Athenians built the Parthenon on the acropolis (Mars Hill) near their city and dedicated it to Athena, the goddess of wisdom. This was where high-minded intellectuals of the city gathered to endlessly talk philosophy. It is where Paul met with them and delivered one of the greatest speeches recorded in Scripture.[32]

Thus, Paul knew from personal experience about both the Jews and the Greeks in their respective search for wisdom. Paul asserts that neither way is adequate. Look again at what he said. "Jews demand miraculous signs and Greeks look for wisdom, but *we preach Christ crucified: a stumbling block to Jews and foolishness to Gentiles, but to those whom God has called, both Jews and Greeks, Christ the power of God and the wisdom of God*" (1 Corinthians 1:22-25 emphasis mine).

Two thousand years ago Paul understood the futility of both foci. True wisdom can be found in neither. It can only be found in the risen Christ! The so-called "wisdom" of the world is often self-serving and characterized by shrewdness and craftiness. In the dog-eat-dog world of one-upmanship, winning at any cost is the name of the game.

One of the most egregious examples from the world of politics comes from the 2012 campaign for the Presidency of the United States. Senate

---

[32] You can read this story in Acts 17:16-34.

Majority Leader Harry Reid blatantly lied on the Senate floor claiming damning evidence of tax evasion by Republican candidate Mitt Romney. The charge was completely false, but after Democrat Barak Obama won the election, a journalist confronted Reid about lying to the Senate and the American electorate. Reid smugly replied with a little self-congratulating smirk, "But Mitt Romney didn't win, did he?" Arrogance personified in the "wisdom" of the world!

Success for the Jews of Paul's day was seeing proof in the form of miracles they could see and touch, affirming their own rightness as God's chosen people. The message of a crucified Messiah simply couldn't satisfy that need. To them, the Rabbi from Nazareth was a total failure who deserved to die. And, in their way, the Greeks agreed. Call death on a Roman cross a victory? Preposterous! Death is not victory. Death in battle means total defeat.

In the middle of that argument, Paul declares with pointed force, "You're both wrong. The crucified Christ is the ultimate source of both power and wisdom!"

Contrast those Jewish and Greek ideas of wisdom—so-called—with the statements of biblical prophets who understood the real truth:

1.   "The fear of the Lord is the beginning of wisdom, and the knowledge of the Holy One is understanding" (Proverbs 9:10).

2.　　"If any of you lacks wisdom, he should ask of God . . . and it will be given to him" (James 1:5).

3.　　"To each [believer] the manifestation of the Spirit is given for the common good . . . the message of wisdom" (1 Corinthians 12:7-8).

4.　　"The Spirit of the Lord will rest on him—that is, the "Branch," i.e. the "Messiah,"—the Spirit of wisdom and understanding" (Isaiah 11:2).

The prophet's major point: *Wisdom is a (spiritual) gift from God.*

The Bible tells of numerous individuals gifted with incredible wisdom. Two who immediately come to mind are the Old Testament stories of Joseph[33] and Daniel.[34]

Joseph—the favorite, spoiled son of the Patriarch Jacob— was sold into slavery by his ten jealous brothers. He is subsequently transported to Egypt and acquired in the slave market by a high official named Potiphar. Potiphar's wife thinks this young Hebrew slave looks pretty good and tries to seduce him. Joseph refuses, and as a result, gets

---

[33] Joseph's story can be found in Genesis 37ff.

[34] Read about Daniel's experience in Daniel 1-2.

thrown into prison. There, he conducts himself with such honesty and integrity that he is made overseer of all the other prisoners.

One night, two of those fellow prisoners each have a strange dream which they believe must carry significant meaning, and they ask Joseph about their dreams. God gives Joseph supernatural insight to interpret the dreams, which proves to be prophetically accurate.

A full two years later, Pharaoh— the king of Egypt—also had two dreams he could not understand. His personal butler—one of the prison dreamers—suddenly remembers how Joseph was able to interpret his dream in prison. Pharaoh calls for Joseph, who comes, listens to Pharaoh's description of the dreams, and tells him the meaning: seven years of plenty lie ahead for Egypt, followed by another seven years of drought and famine.

Joseph counsels Pharaoh to use the next seven years to prepare for the years of famine to follow. Pharaoh thinks that it is a good idea and appoints Joseph as Prime Minister of Egypt to oversee the task of storing grain so the people can survive the upcoming years of want. The kicker comes when Joseph's brothers appear before him hoping to buy grain.

The famine has extended far north into the lands where Jacob and his family live as nomadic shepherds. The brothers do not recognize Joseph, but he immediately knows them. Some interesting events transpire, and in the end Jacob and all his household move to Egypt so they can survive the famine.

Woven throughout the entire story of Joseph is a golden thread of integrity and wisdom. I believe it started as Joseph—the newly purchased prisoner-slave—gazed at his father's tents as the caravan traveled toward Egypt.

The ancient trade route from Damascus in Syria to Memphis in Egypt ran south along the eastern shore of the Mediterranean Sea through what we know today as the Gaza Strip. At the beginning of Joseph's story, he found his brothers pasturing the family flocks in northern Galilee. Their father's main camp was far to the South in the Negev. When the camel caravan passed the place where the brothers were camped, they saw a convenient opportunity to get Joseph out of their lives and proceeded to sell him to the traders.

On the journey south the caravan passed to the west of Jacob's tents. The young Joseph gazed at his home encampment in the distance and realized he may never see his father or other family members again. He had no idea what his immediate future would bring. It isn't a stretch to think he must have experienced extreme confusion, grief, and fear. And, yet, as he peered across the desert toward the only home he had ever known, he resolved that regardless of what might happen to him in the future he would be true to the teachings of his father, and he would continue to worship only the God of his father Jacob.

Joseph made a wise choice. God honored his choice and blessed him with favor through the rest of his life as he continued to serve those around him with true dignity, honor, and respect.

Daniel has a similar story from (roughly) a thousand years later.

A young Hebrew prince is captured along with many of his fellow countrymen, and marched across the desert from Jerusalem to Babylon in 605 B.C. Daniel along with three other young captives were selected for training in the "University of Babylon" in all the language and literature of Babylon's culture. King Nebuchadnezzar wanted these young Hebrews to serve in the palace. He recognized their outstanding aptitude and promise and instructed the chief of the court officials to give them the best of food and other Babylonian delicacies as part of their training. Nebuchadnezzar truly believed he was giving them every advantage to excel.

But the four Hebrew youth knew that the king's meats and wines would dull their senses and weaken their bodies. They bargained with the steward in charge of their care to let them try their own diet of vegetables and water for ten days, then determine the results.

It worked!

The story says, "At the end of the ten days they looked healthier and better nourished than any of the young men who ate the royal food. So the guard took away their choice food and the wine they were to drink and gave them vegetables instead" (Daniel 1:15-16).

As in Joseph's story, the foundational choice these young men made at the beginning of their experience in an entirely foreign and potentially hostile culture made all the difference for the rest of their lives.

Sometime later, King Nebuchadnezzar also had a divine dream, but he had no idea what it meant, and he couldn't even remember the details. He was sure it was of great importance, however. When none of the soothsayers or magicians could tell him the dream or what it might mean, the king flew into a rage and ordered that they all be killed, and their houses destroyed!

When Daniel heard about this, he arranged to ask the king for some time to pray with his friends about the matter. He and his friends prayed to God to reveal the dream and its message.

Nebuchadnezzar agreed to their request. They prayed. God answered, and Daniel was able to deliver the message of four great world empires coming in the future—Babylon, Medo-Persia, Greece, and Rome—symbolized by the image of a man made of different metals—gold, silver, bronze, and iron.

Before Daniel delivered the revelation of the dream and its meaning to Nebuchadnezzar, he praised God, saying, "[You] give wisdom to the wise and knowledge to the discerning" (Daniel 2:21). Then, when he stood before the king he prefaced his message, "No wise man, enchanter magician or diviner can explain to the king the mystery he has asked about, but there is a God in heaven who reveals mysteries. He has shown King Nebuchadnezzar what will happen in the days to come" (Daniel 2:27).

Joseph and Daniel are just two examples of individuals who received wisdom and understanding from the Holy Spirit of God. The Bible, and indeed the entire history of humanity is filled with many similar stories as God guided them through challenging or uncertain times.

We can trust God to give those same gifts to us in our times of need.

King Solomon who reigned during the apex of Israel's glory days declared, "Blessed is the [person] who finds wisdom, the [one] who gains understanding, for [wisdom] is more profitable than silver and yields better returns than gold" (Proverbs 3:13-14).

The Bible teaches clearly that true wisdom is a gift from a God desiring the best for his children. Holy Spirit-given wisdom inspires positive thinking and enables good choices. While the wisdom of the world tends to self-serving and self-centered efforts of personal promotion, the wisdom of God is self-sacrificing and focused on service to others.

This wisdom from on high is freely available to those who ask for it. That's why my sixth essential daily prayer is "Wisdom for My Counsel: *That the Fear of the Lord Might ever be My Guide.*"

As Solomon said, "The fear of the Lord is the beginning of wisdom, and knowledge of the Holy One is understanding" (Proverbs 9:10).

Study Guide

Chapter 6 "Wisdom for My Counsel"

True Wisdom follows neither the Capricious Fads of Populism nor the Immobility of Frozen Traditionalism

---

1. How much weight do you put on apparent miracles as proof that God exists, or that unexplained

healings give evidence of God's favor?

2. Do you see "truth" more through the lenses of emotion or logic? Why? Explain.

3. What are some challenges you face which test your integrity? How might you be struggling with hypocrisy, even though you may not be fully aware of it in your own life?

4. The stories of Joseph and Daniel are great biblical examples of individuals with great wisdom. Who else can you cite as truly wise? Your list could include other biblical characters, historical figures, or persons who are currently alive. How does their example inspire you to emulate them in making healthy, wise choices?

Your Thoughts:

Chapter Seven

To Be a Godly Influence in the World

That My Life Will Only Count for God's Eternal Kingdom

By faith Able offered God a better sacrifice than Cain did. By faith he was commended as a righteous man, when God spoke well of his offerings. And by faith he still speaks, even though he is dead (Hebrews 11:4).

I hang my head in shame when I recall some of my words and actions in the once-upon-a-time unchangeable past. I feel even worse when I think about the effect my attitudes and conduct may have had on friends and fellow travelers. So many times my influence was wrong-headed—definitely anything but righteous. For years I tried intensely to maintain a surface facade of being a good kid, especially around adults and girls. But just under the surface my life was full of trash and self-centered pride. All the guys I ran with knew who I really was. The others probably did too. I suspect my "cover" was far more transparent than I imagined. Truth be told, I didn't actually think about it. I just acted differently around different sets of people. I seem to have been a bonafide hypocrite and didn't even know it!

But one night God turned his powerful spotlight on all that inner ugliness and brought me to my knees. At that moment I knew my only hope was to confess my sins and plead for forgiveness. The Bible says, "If we confess our sins, he is faithful and just and will forgive us our sins and purify us from all unrighteousness" (1 John 1:9).

What a great promise! My gratitude is truly beyond words.

But, here's the thing: While God's grace and forgiveness are worthy of celebration, the fruit of our words and actions doesn't just go away. The influences generated from long-forgotten events never cease to ripple across the social waters of our world. Every day we toss new "pebbles" into the "pond." Every wave from every pebble becomes a force of influence that touches every person in its path. The effects can—and often do—last for generations. The energy of those waves cannot be stopped or recalled. Once in motion, they will continue their journey, constantly passing on the good or evil fruit they carry.

Consider this.

In the pre-dawn darkness of a Southwest Missouri Civil War morning a tiny newborn scrap of humanity—stuffed into a burlap bag and tied to the back of a saddle—is tossed roughly into the hands of a slave-owning German immigrant named Moses. The nameless baby and his mother Mary had been stolen days earlier in a night-time raid, possibly by a band of the infamous Quantrill's Raiders, aka Confederate "bushwhackers" who carried out guerrilla attacks on civilian targets in Missouri and Kansas.

Through an intermediary, Moses attempted to negotiate the return of his slave Mary and her child, promising to trade his prized stallion in exchange.

Sadly, the rendezvous and transaction did not go as planned. Mary was not with the raiders when they arrived at the meeting place. The bushwhackers took the stallion and then shot Moses's wagon mare in the head, killing her instantly. One of the men threw the burlap bag in Moses's general direction then followed his gang as they galloped off into the night. In a desperate stretch, Moses strained to catch the bag before it hit the ground. Opening it, he discovered a tiny infant still alive.

It was Mary's baby. He immediately opened his coat and placed the child next to his bare skin, warming him and protecting him from the elements. Clutching the baby to his chest, Farmer Moses began the long walk home.

When the war ended in 1865—and the slaves now free—Moses and his wife Susan decided to formally adopt the little boy and his older brother James so they could raise them as their own. They loved the boys and wanted to give them every advantage available for Negro children in the post-war years. They named the younger brother in honor of an American President whom they greatly admired and gave him their own last name. That little throw-away slave child would forever afterward be known as George Washington Carver.[35]

George W. Carver's accomplishments in life are the stuff of legend. Eventually, he taught for 47 years at Booker T. Washington's Tuskegee Institute (now Tuskegee University). His experiments with peanuts and sweet potatoes, methods of crop rotation, and other improvements revolutionized agriculture in the South. By the time of his death on January 5, 1943, George's fame had spread far and wide. In 1941 *Time* Magazine labeled him "a Black Leonardo." He is one of the truly great people in

---

[35] This story is a condensed portion of a much longer, more detailed account told by author Andy Andrews in *The Lost Choice: A Legend of Personal Discovery.* Nelson Books: A Division of Thomas Nelson Publishers, 2004.

American history, and one of the most powerful positive influences of modern times.

The question can legitimately be asked, Where would our culture be today without the likes of George Washington Carver?

Behind that question, however, is a deeper, more fundamental issue. Where would George Washington Carver have been without the love and nurture of his adoptive parents, Moses and Susan Carver? Even before that, how would history have been different if Moses Carver hadn't saved the life of that tiny, insignificant slave baby one terrible night in war-ravaged Southwest Missouri? Suffice it to say, it was the Carvers' heart—the influence of their life—that formed the foundation of character, combined with a thirst for knowledge, which produced the fruit of their son's life work. Without Moses and Susan Carver, there would be no George Washington Carver. Without George Washington Carver, we all would be the poorer.

Influence is a most powerful factor in human relationships.

In some rare moments we may occasionally know when our presence has made a significant difference in another person's life. Most times we have no idea. It might be days or even years later—if ever at all—that we discover how our life touched another life with significance.

In the summer of 1964, I was nineteen years old. I spent most of that summer selling children's Bible storybooks around Salem, Oregon. Whenever I had a free weekend, I often headed north on Interstate-5 to Portland to visit a certain student nurse working in the hospital there. She and I had a lot of fun together. We enjoyed getting better acquainted each time we got together.

On one visit Mary[36] told me she would be going home in a couple of weeks and invited me to go with her so I could meet her parents. That sounded great to me! I rather liked where this friendship might be leading. The trip involved a long, all-day trip on a Greyhound bus, followed by another three hours by car from the town where Mary's mother met the bus to pick us up. I was a happy camper, getting to spend all this time with the young lady I enjoyed.

We did indeed have a great weekend. Her parents were friendly and welcomed me with open arms. They were farm folk, so I felt entirely comfortable in their home. Somewhere along the way I got an invitation to sing special music for their church worship service. I agreed, and Mary accompanied me on the piano. I sang a simple little hymn of fellowship with God as my closest friend. Everyone seemed to enjoy the music. And that was that.

---

[36] Not her real name.

The weekend visit came to an end. Mary and I returned to our jobs in Oregon, but not long after that our lives turned in different directions. Nevertheless, I still carried wonderful memories of that fun-filled summer, and life moved on.

Years passed—many years.

Over twenty years later I had occasion to speak as a guest pastor in that same little church. Very few of the "old-timers" were there who might remember that one lone visit and the song I sang for special music that day. But one of the older members approached me after my sermon.

"Do you remember singing special music when you were here at that time?" she asked.

"Yes, of course!" I answered.

"Well, I just wanted you to know what a profound impression you made on my son. He was eight or nine years old back then. He really loved the song you shared, and for years afterward he practiced and practiced. He always said, 'I want to be able to sing just like Loren Fenton!'"

Talk about a humbling experience! What a wake-up call!

I don't think my "special music" was particularly memorable that day, but a young boy in that tiny congregation was influenced for years afterward because of my song.

Little, seemingly insignificant moments do make a difference in the life of people we encounter every day. You never know what a wave, a smile, a word of encouragement, or a pat on the back might do to lift someone's day. Only God can trace the effect of our presence in this world. We will never know the whole story until we get into his eternal Kingdom.

Jesus says in Matthew 12:36 that we will be judged by every little word we say, whether it is good or evil. The verdict of this judgment is directly tied to the influence of our words on the life of the people around us. Do our communications result in encouragement, hope, and peace, or do they produce discouragement, despair, and anger? That idea could be terrifying to the point of sleepless nights! Who hasn't inadvertently said something that caused distress for someone else, even if that was never our intention? God help us!

Ah, but the good news is—God *does* help us! Not only does he forgive the sins and blunders of our past, but by his grace he also empowers us to grow daily more and more into his likeness—to be like him.

Being like Christ begins with our mental choices. Our "Christ-likeness" is measured by our relationships and how we treat the people around us. We choose to live by faith that the Holy Spirit will flow through us to touch the lives of others with his saving, redeeming, sustaining grace.

The Judgment is good news to those who are *in Christ.* "There is now no condemnation for those who are in Christ Jesus" (Romans 8:1).

Why is there no condemnation? Two reasons:

1.   One, the sinless life record of Jesus is given to us as we accept his offer in exchange for our blemished record.

2.   Second, when we are "in Christ," and Christ is "in us," we relate to others in positive, life-giving appreciation for who they are as individual human beings. We become more sensitive to the needs of other people, and we gradually learn how to respond to those needs in a Christ-like manner.

What do you want to leave as a legacy when you die?

In his book *First Things First,*[37] Dr. Stephen Covey identifies four basic human needs: to live, to love, to learn, and to leave a legacy. By the single simple fact of living in this world every individual leaves a mark. We have no choice about that. But

---

[37] Covey, Stephen R., A. Roger Merrill, Rebecca R. Merrill; *First Things First: To Live, to Love, to Learn, to Leave a Legacy*; Simon & Schuster, New York NY, 1994.

we do have a choice about the content of our legacy, aka the influence we behind. Will that influence be for better or for worse? That is the question.

Our influence is the only thing we leave in this world. Everything else is transitory. A few generations pass and the memorable moments of individual lives fade into genealogy listings of vital statistics found only in dusty corners of obscure heritage libraries. Yet, the influence of our personal choices continues to live on through succeeding generations—sometimes with incredible power.

Look at this text from Hebrews 11:4 — "By faith Abel offered God a better sacrifice than Cain did. By faith he was commended as a righteous man, when God spoke well of his offerings. And by faith, he still speaks, even though he is dead."

And this from 2 Corinthians 9:2 — "I know your eagerness to help, and I have been boasting about it to the Macedonians, telling them that since last year you in Achaia were ready to give; and your enthusiasm has stirred most of them to action."

The Bible also gives examples of powerful influences for evil. For example, in his first letter to the Corinthians, Paul writes, "Your boasting is not good. Don't you know that a little yeast works through the whole batch of dough?" (1 Corinthians 5:6).

And again, a few chapters later, "Be careful . . . that the exercise of your freedom does not become a stumbling block to the weak" (1 Corinthians 8:9).

The Book of Genesis tells several multi-generational examples of negative influence.

In the account of Cain's descendants[38] the story climaxes with Lamech, Cain's fifth-generation grandson. Lamech is the first individual who took two wives, then boasts to them about his ultra-conceited prowess as a murderer. The heritage from his ancestor Cain—who murdered his brother Able—has multiplied from generation to generation until it breaks out in this evil fruit of self-worshiping rebellion.

Another example comes following the story of Noah and the Flood.

The genealogical lines diverge again into lines of good and evil—specifically couched in the descendants of Shem, contrasted with that of his brothers Ham and Japheth. The "mighty warrior" Nimrod[39] was a grandson of Ham. Nimrod built the foundations of Babylon and other cultures which became the archenemies of Shem's descendants—the Semitic peoples—who were loyal to the worship of the Creator God. The influences of these ancients are still with us today! Just look at the never-ending conflicts in the Middle East!

---

[38] Genesis 4:17-24.

[39] Genesis 10:8-11.

But, before we get too mired in the muck of negativity, let's turn our eyes to some reasons for hope. People can—and do—change via the power of the living Christ!

In the chapter, "Wisdom for My Counsel," I quoted the Apostle Paul writing, "Jews demand miraculous signs and Greeks look for wisdom, but we preach Christ crucified: a stumbling block to Jews and foolishness to Gentiles, but to those whom God has called, both Jews and Greeks, Christ the power of God and the wisdom of God" (1 Corinthians 1:22-25).

I can tell you from my own experience, God does change the trajectory of people—not just of individuals, but also of families through generation after generation.

You already know that severe alcoholism virtually destroyed my father's family of origin when his father—my grandfather Arthur Fenton— abandoned his wife and children to chase a bottle for the next several decades.[40] But the roots of this problem reached back at least one more generation to Arthur's father, and perhaps beyond.

The American Civil War created profound influences in the Fenton family line. During that terrible conflict Thomas W. Fenton—my great-grandfather—enlisted in the Iowa Infantry. Thomas was wounded in the right leg during the Battle of

---

[40] See Chapter 5, "Strength for My Body," section on "Temperance."

Mark's Mills not far south of Little Rock, Arkansas. The entire Iowa 36th regiment was either killed, wounded, or captured, and taken as prisoners-of-war to Camp Ford, Tyler, Texas.

When the war was over Thomas returned north to Iowa and married a young woman named Amelia Martin—his second wife. Amelia tragically died a few years later giving birth to their fourth child. Thomas and Amelia's third son, my grandfather Arthur, was two-and-a-half years old at the time of his mother's death.

The obvious emotional pain of losing two wives, the trauma of war—including those terrible months of confinement in the Confederate POW camp—and the heavy responsibility of raising three very young sons by himself created incredible stress in Thomas's life.

Following his wife's death, Thomas moved his family to a farm in Southwest Missouri near the town of Butler. His mother and an unmarried sister also made the move. They were needed to help care for the three motherless boys.

Unfortunately, Aunt Lide (Eliza)—by all accounts—was a very mean person who constantly punished the growing boys, showing them no mercy for even the slightest missteps. Her unloving, hard discipline instilled a deep-seated anger-depression the boys carried with them through the rest of their life. One tragic result was the eventual murder-suicide by Edward, the oldest brother, who killed his wife in a drunken rage, and then turned the gun on himself.

When my grandfather Arthur ran away from his family, my grandmother Hattie had no choice but to "farm her children out" to foster families willing to take them in. Claude (age 11) went to live with a family named Leibecker somewhere in the Palouse Country of Eastern Washington. By the time Claude was sixteen years old he was on his own, working for a variety of ranchers around the region. At the outbreak of WWI, he enlisted in the US Marine Corps and spent two years stationed at Guantanamo Bay in Cuba.

As I mentioned in the previous chapter, my father absolutely refused to have anything to do with alcohol in any form, even in his years as a US Marine and as a ranch hand in the rough conditions of life on Eastern Washington ranches. His unbending stand and example became a major influence for me and my siblings.

One of my daily prayers now for my entire extended family is that they can always stay free from this curse. The demon alcohol has not been good to us. I pray it will never again raise its ugly head.

Mark this down. YOUR influence can change the direction of another person's life and can continue generations into the future. By turning the power, effects, and extent of your influence over to God, you can be certain that it will only be used for good to accomplish His purposes. By your choices—and through the empowerment of God's grace—YOU can turn the tide of evil to leave a legacy of life, hope, healing, and encouragement.

Now, I must bring all this to a close by telling you about three individuals whose combined influence totally changed the direction of my life. Because of these three my walk with God came alive in ways I never knew before. Each served a separate purpose, but each merged seamlessly into God's master plan for me. Fused by the Holy Spirit they formed the very nucleus of my entire life and ministry that yet lay in my future.

I have chosen to use their real names because I am eternally grateful for how their lives impacted mine. I share them here to honor what they did for me. Many others could be included, but here are three people who created a pivotal shift in my life's journey.

Doris Matson was the youth leader for our church family all through my growing-up years. She began teaching our cohort of church kids in Kindergarten, then followed us as we graduated to Primary, then Juniors, and on into the teenage Youth class. Doris's long-term love inspired her devotion as our teacher and group mother, even after some of our group moved on to college, got married, or otherwise launched into adult living. She was always there for us—encouraging, supporting, sharing, inspiring, and wise.

Doris and her husband Merlin were just great people with a super-abundance of love for kids. Saturday nights often found us crowded into their home for popcorn, group games, and good times. We made a host of great memories.

Doris and Merlin's ministry made our youth group inspirational and fun. They helped us study the Bible, coached us as student leaders, and counseled as we organize our own events. They didn't just plan things for us to do. They opened the door and let us create our own vision of Christian living—all while giving invaluable guidance and focus. They never preached their values. They just lived them. Their counsel was pure gold.

The Matsons' influence in our youth group—and specifically for me—was truly profound. It was the first of three powerful streams converging during my teen years bringing me to my knees and a true conversion to Christ.

The second was a high school friend I met by sheer coincidence.[41]

Bonita Etulain sat beside me in our high school Latin class. Seats were assigned in rigid alphabetical order. Her last name began with "E," mine with "F." We occupied the two last desks at

---

[41] Is there really such a thing as pure coincidence? I don't think so! God is the great director of circumstances in life. He opens doors and orchestrates relationships to achieve his purposes.

the end of the very front row of seats in the classroom.

At the beginning of my sophomore year I had no idea how much Bonita—one year older than me—would impact my life. Her influence that year opened the second major spiritual stream merging into my experience. I didn't know it then, but God was right in the middle of this relationship working out his purpose for my future.

By all accounts I should have been in our high school's Vocational Agriculture (VoAg) class instead of Latin. It was widely assumed—and pretty much expected—that high school boys from our farming community would enroll in VoAg and join Future Farmers of America (FFA). As a freshman (9th grade) I had followed the customary path. But when 10th grade rolled around I made a very strange decision.

From the early age of five I had my sights set on becoming a veterinarian. In some sort of quirky thinking I decided that learning Latin would help me prepare for college training in veterinary medicine much more than VoAg or FFA.

My VoAg teacher certainly didn't see it that way, but he reluctantly signed my transfer request.

Academically, it was without a doubt one of the biggest mistakes of my entire formal education. I ended that year of Latin by totally failing the class! Nevertheless, I have realized in later years that God's hand was guiding me, even then. Despite the disastrous outcome of that year, God placed me exactly where I needed to be for the new path forward he had ordained for me to follow.

Our Latin teacher Mr. Moga often provided quiet periods in class for us to study the language's grammar, vocabulary, etc. No talking allowed! Stay focused! During one of these quiet study times I sneaked a glance over to Bonita's desk to see what she was doing. I was surprised to see her memorizing Scripture verses on flashcards—not studying Latin!

Our public school included students from many faith backgrounds. I didn't know Bonita well at that point. I had no idea what church she and her family attended.

I quickly scribbled a note and slipped it onto her desk. "Why are you memorizing Bible texts?" I asked.

She wrote back, "It's for a Bible Bowl competition in YFC."

"YFC?" I responded. "What is that?" I guessed it must be the initials for her church's youth ministry.

"Youth for Christ," she answered. "You should come."

"Is that the name of your church youth group?"

"No, YFC is a Christian club for teens from any church. Everyone can be part of it. It doesn't matter what church you're from. We have a meeting this Friday after school at the Nazarene Church. Would you like to come?"

"Yes, I would," I quickly wrote my reply. "That sounds interesting."

The Nazarene Church building was right across the street from our high school. The next Friday I walked over to the church instead of getting on my bus to go home. Bonita and several other young people were already there.

"Hi, Loren! Welcome to YFC!" Everyone seemed excited to see me walk in the door.

That was the beginning of my involvement with Youth for Christ, an evangelical movement sharing the gospel with high school teens everywhere. I began attending the weekly meetings regularly and went with Bonita to monthly YFC rallies in Yakima, the "big city" of our county about 35 miles away. The next year I served as vice-president for our local club, and the following year—my senior year—I was elected president. During Christmas break in my junior year I attended YFC's "Capitol Teen Convention" in Washington, D.C with approximately 12,000 other teenagers from all around the United States. One of the featured speakers was Billy Graham who addressed the gathering in person, along with many famous Christian sports stars, entertainers, and political personalities.

The focus of every YFC event—from our local club meetings to the regional rallies to the great national gatherings—was an invitation for every "unsaved" young person to accept Jesus Christ and his gift of eternal life. Not even training meetings for new club leaders or group recreational activities were exempt. Salvation by grace through faith permeated every thought, every plan, and every organizational body in YFC. Saving kids for eternity was—and is—YFC's continuing *raison d'être.*

My experience with Youth for Christ opened a door in my heart I had not fully understood before. My childhood church spoke often of grace and faith, but the heaviest emphasis was always on Obedience (with a capital "O"). God's Law was supreme. God's grace seemed secondary. But the light of God's love and grace shone brightly into my life through the ministry of YFC. It was through them I learned to walk with Jesus as my personal Savior and Lord.

This second stream of influence (salvation by grace through faith alone) blended perfectly with the first (positive social Christian fellowship).

The third stream arrived right on time—just when both of the others were in full force.

Evangelist Don Gray and his team came to our town (Sunnyside, Washington) with a big bubble tent in 1960 at the start of my sophomore year, and roughly the same time I began my involvement with Youth for Christ.

One October afternoon my friend Dale gave me a ride home after school. Dale drove north out of downtown Sunnyside on North 6th Street. As we neared the intersection of North 6th and what is now called Yakima Valley Highway, I suddenly saw this big air-supported tent pitched in a vacant lot on the east side of the street. It was huge!

"Oh, wow!" I shouted. "Look at that!"

Dale was busy driving and didn't see what I was so excited about.

"Turn around!" I said. "I want to see it better!"

Dale obliged and maneuvered to go back so we could get a better look. A large sign in front of the tent read, "BIBLE PROPHECY MEETINGS" giving the date of the opening night of an upcoming series of Bible lectures.

"That's really cool! I want to go to those meetings!"

Dale chuckled at my enthusiasm, but I was serious. Opening night saw me—along with a couple of hundred other people—crowded into the tent.

The interior was filled with rows and rows of chairs facing the speaker's wooden platform in the front. A large booth stood at the back of the room housing movie and slide projectors. A giant screen mounted behind the platform displayed beautiful nature scenes while the people entered, then was used to show Bible quotations and illustrations for the sermon. A grand piano and an electric organ flanked the platform. Beautiful gospel music flooded the room. It was awesome! I was "in heaven."

The organizers of the meetings had an attendance incentive feature in place. A person attending 25 of the 30 scheduled meetings could receive a brand-new Bible as a thank-you gift. I was determined to get my Bible. I didn't have one of my own and this was a good opportunity. It was a happy moment when I got my 25th hole punched in the record card and I took possession of my very own new King James Bible.

I learned a lot from attending Evangelist Gray's Bible lectures. He had a nightly travelogue with home movies and color slides he had personally taken on a recent trip around the world. He told fascinating stories linking ancient history and current events relevant to the nations and cultures he visited, and how they fit into the biblical prophecies of end times.

On one evening toward the end of the series, Evangelist Gray showed a beautiful picture of Christ with hands outstretched in the invitation. The appeal stirred my heart, and I went forward together with several other people. We were ushered to a small area at the back of the platform where several chairs had been placed to accommodate the seekers. After we were seated the evangelist spoke to us from his heart about our walk with God.

"I have two Bible texts to share with you," he began. "I encourage you to memorize these texts and underline them in your Bible."

He then had us open our Bibles.

"The first text is 1 John 1:7," he said. "Here it is: *If we walk in the light, as he is in the light, we have fellowship one with another, and the blood of Jesus Christ his Son cleanseth us from all sin.*"

"The second text is very similar, and it is only two verses later in the same chapter. It is 1 John 1:9: *If we confess our sins, he is faithful and just to forgive us our sins, and to cleanse us from all unrighteousness.*[42]"

I never forgot that moment or those two texts. They have bolstered my faith time and time again through all the many years since.

Several months passed after I responded to that call. It was nearly a year later in the early weeks of the next school year—Fall of 1961—when I walked out under the stars and opened my heart fully to God.[43]

Then the journey began.

---

[42] Both texts quoted here are from the KJV.

[43] Read my conversion story in the Introduction at the beginning of this book.

The journey continues still.

God is faithful.

God is good.

I have only recently realized the role each of these powerful streams of witness played in bringing me to that point of submission and confession.

- The ministry of Doris and Merlin Matson—combined with a vibrant youth fellowship in my home church—provided an essential positive social environment to anchor my nascent personal walk with God.

- The faithful Christian witness of Bonita Etulain who drew me into involvement with Youth for Christ where my heart was opened more fully to the gospel of salvation by grace through faith.

- The Spirit-filled, Bible-based teaching of Evangelist Don Gray whose presence brought timely instruction in Bible truths, a Christian understanding of history, and a sharpened awareness of last-day events as foretold by the ancient prophetic words of Scripture.

The memory of these dear friends continues to energize my faith and empower my devotion to

Christ even now, nearly sixty years hence. And thus, I pray every day that *my* influence will rightly represent the King I serve, touching the lives of others with life, hope, healing, and encouragement.

Study Guide

Chapter Seven "To Be a Godly Influence in the World"

When We Come to the End of our Earthly Life, the Only Thing We Leave Behind is our Influence, Whether for Good or Evil

1. What can you do to ensure that your influence today will only count for God's Kingdom?

2. How can you connect with people who are part of your daily routines

with more than mere surface relationships?

3. In what ways can you carry "sunshine" into your world, even for those with whom you have only momentary contact?

4. List several mediums of communication that you can effectively use to deliver positive messages of encouragement.

5. Create a list of people who have significantly influenced your faith. How did each one touch your life with God's grace? What steps can you take to let them know your appreciation? When will you do it?

6. How will you emulate the grace shown to you by the people you listed in question five?

Your Thoughts:

Chapter Eight

Building the Firewall

Establishing My Seven Essential Daily Prayers *as a Daily Habit*[44]

How can a young man keep his way pure? By living according to your word. I seek you with all my heart; do not

---

[44] The bulk of this chapter is taken from a book I wrote and published in 1977. *Thirteen Weeks to Riches: Which Could Be Glory* was my first attempt at writing and self-publishing a book. The last chapter in *Thirteen Weeks* was titled "Daily Growth." I have adapted and updated some of the content here. I have a limited number of the original *Thirteen Weeks* books available at https://lorenfentonauthor.com/store

let me stray from your commands. I have hidden your word in my heart that I might not sin against you (Psalm 119:9-11).

One day I was at a special conference that was studying the subject of prayer. The speaker was a retired minister about seventy years old. He had more spark and energy than I've seen in many men much younger! His secret was a divine enthusiasm for life.

Pastor Glenn Coon told of his experience when he left home to attend college. His father, a godly man, took him to the railroad station. Before they parted, they had prayer together, then his father gave him this advice: Spend at least one hour every day with the Lord—no matter what.

When Glenn arrived at the college, he got a job milking cows on the college farm. He had to leave for work at 4:00 a.m. A busy school program kept him quite busy with classes and study until quite late at night, so to get his "hour with the Lord" he had to get up at 3:00 a.m. He did this faithfully every morning all during his college years.

At the prayer conference Pastor Coon told me, "I have continued the habit of spending an hour with God every morning. Not always at 3:00 a.m., but every morning before anything else has a chance to interrupt. My time with the Lord has always had the highest priority. It is this habit— more than anything else—that has energized my life and given me the strength I need every day."

When I heard Pastor Coon make this testimony I was inspired to follow his example. I set my alarm clock for a half-hour earlier than my normal wake-up time. The following morning' I headed downstairs to my den. I was excited to begin this new adventure in prayer. I closed and locked the door behind me and sat down at my desk.

Only then did I feel the enormity of my ignorance. I realized at that moment I had no idea how I could ever spend a full hour in communion with God.

"Lord," I prayed, "teach me what I should do here now. I admit, I don't know what to do or say."

As I prayed those words the thought flashed through my mind that part of prayer is Bible study—and good Christian reading material. So I decided to try dividing the hour into three 20-minute segments: the first twenty minutes for reading; the second period for Bible study; and the third for prayer.

Behind me on the wall was a whole library of books and other miscellaneous reading materials. I picked out a book I'd been wanting to read for some time, opened it, and began my journey.

At the end of the allotted time I put in a page marker and set the book in a special place on my desk and turned my attention to the Bible.

How to study it?

I had read the Bible through from cover to cover a couple of times already. I didn't want to do the same thing over again. I wanted variety.

I couldn't think of any special way to study the Bible that morning, so I decided just to read the New Testament in a modern translation. That would be a change. I picked up *Today's English Version* (TEV). I'd been wanting to read it for a long time.

What a thrill it was reading the TEV that morning! At the end of twenty minutes I could hardly put it down. But I forced myself to put in a marker and place it next to the first book on my desk.

Now came the real trial. How could I spend an entire twenty minutes on my knees? Twenty minutes! That block of time seemed as formidable as a fortress. Previously, I had never been able to spend even five minutes in prayer without getting bored.

But now, here I was. The time had come.

I pushed my chair back and knelt before my desk.

"Lord," I prayed again, "I don't know how to pray like this. Help me know—and help me to pray the way you want me to."

I didn't hear any trumpets or audible voices, but once again I heard in my spirit the same voice that spoke to me on that dusty farm road the night I opened my heart to God.[45] I recognized his voice immediately. The Holy Spirit directed my thoughts to Jesus teaching his disciples to pray.

Still on my knees, I reached over and got my Bible and turned to the Lord's Prayer.[46] As I studied this model prayer, I saw that it was divided into three major parts: praise; requests; and praise.

So, that's my trouble! I thought. *All I've ever done in prayer is making requests. What I need to do is begin and end my prayer with praise!*

I closed my eyes again and started to praise the Lord.

But the thought crossed my mind, *what should I praise him for? Isn't praise supposed to be thanksgiving for blessings received?*

How typical! Far too often our center is not God, but ourselves! "What has he done for me?" is the question we're always asking. It's as self-centered as can be!

Then it came to my mind that our praise of God—our worship of him—doesn't depend on whether he has done anything for us or not. We

---

[45] This story is included in the Introduction at the beginning of this book.

[46] Matthew 6:9-13

should worship him and praise him because he is *worthy* of worship. He is *worthy* of praise.

As this great truth permeated my thoughts that first morning, I couldn't contain my joy. Kneeling there at my desk I raised my hands high into the air, palms opened and arms wide to praise the Lord. As I did this an overpowering sense of love and awe swept over my entire being. I held onto that joy and tried to prolong it. I didn't have to contribute anything—just to be there in his presence and worship him was enough!

In a few moments I remembered some personal issues I needed to present to the Lord. I spoke them aloud and then thanked him for answering these needs according to his wisdom and love. I ended my prayer time with another session of praise and worship.

I looked at my watch. My twenty minutes were just finishing. I hadn't been bored at all! It was a thrilling experience—one I wouldn't trade for anything.

But I must sound one note of caution. If you are looking for a wonderful experience with God, you must not make *the experience* primary. You must make *God himself* the object of your adoration and praise. We must not worship the experience we seek. Instead we must worship our great Creator God. He—and he alone—is worthy of worship.

We have covered a lot of ground in these seven chapters. Purity, righteousness, integrity, joy, strength, wisdom, and influence. I truly pray that the thoughts I shared on these pages may have been an encouragement and a blessing to you. My purpose here is to inspire faith in the great God of heaven who does hear and does answer our personal prayers. If my sharing can in some small way contribute to another person's spiritual growth, I will be most rewarded.

Study Guide

Chapter Eight
"Building the Firewall"

A Habit of Personal Devotions at the Beginning of Every Day will Revolutionize your Walk with God

---

1. If you don't already have a time and place for your regular, daily devotional start to the day, where

and when would you be able to begin?

2. How much time do you think you may need as you set up your new morning routine?

3. What time will you target for your daily time with God? Will you need to set your alarm?

4. What have you found works best for you in personal Bible study? Reading the Bible straight through from cover to cover? Following a daily reading plan? Studying subject by subject? Something else?

5. Other than the *Seven Essential Daily Prayers,* are there other major building blocks you need for your spiritual firewall?

Your Thoughts:

About the Author

Loren L. Fenton, D.Min., was born and raised in Washington State, USA. He is a graduate of Sunnyside, Washington High School (1963), Walla Walla University (1967), and Andrews University (1971 and 1998). Throughout his lifetime he has been a pastor, evangelist, missionary, husband, father, and grandfather.

Loren and his wife Ruth have two children and five grandchildren. They have lived in Washington, Oregon, California, Michigan, West Virginia, Ohio, and Taiwan. They have also toured in China, The Philippines, Israel, Egypt, and many States in the USA. They currently enjoy retirement living in College Place, Washington, where they keep active writing blogs and books, as well as participating in various ministries conducted by their local church.

You can visit Loren's website at
https://LorenFentonAuthor.com

Additional Resources
from
GoodlifeNews! Productions

1) BOOKS by Loren L Fenton available at
   www.amazon.com/author/lorenfenton **or**
   https://LorenFentonAuthor.com

   a) *"Whoa," I Yelled, "Whoa!": A Collection of Stories from My Childhood and Youth.*

   b) *Whimsi and The Big Election.* (Illustrated by Kimberly Holback)

   c) *Thirteen Weeks to Riches: Which Could be Glory*

2) WEBSITES

   a) *https://LorenFentonAuthor.com*

   b) *https://GoodllifeNews.co*

   c) *www.amazon.com/author/lorenfenton*

Made in the USA
Monee, IL
23 June 2020